Syr
Jacl

You … a good time and … l say something … t this one?' You … reassure you by adding, 'I'll get it next time.'

If you pay for my meal and 'do me a favour' –whether with grace or resentment–we have engaged in a symbolic exchange. It's not really about the money; the importance of the gesture is as a sign of trust, friendship and solidarity. The favour is not in any real sense a commercial exchange. It is not at all like a loan, since to get your money back you are forced to go out for dinner with me again (and who knows when 'next time' will be, or if it will come to the same price). Even if every time our meals do cost the same amount, a vital element will be missing from the transaction: the value of the goodwill. You can't put a price on the favour because its worth is measured in social, not financial capital.

Symbolic exchange is, quite simply, where the value of a trade is not monetary but emotional. In other words, it is when the social relationship being established is more important, or has no bearing, on the economic value of what is being traded. It is an exchange that doesn't know, or care about, profit.

When it is one-sided it becomes a form of sacrifice, which is sometimes called a 'symbolic gesture.' The purpose of the symbolic gesture is public and purposeful waste to demonstrate piety. In fact, the bigger the waste (like self-sacrifice), the greater the social standing that results (the tragic hero). Two sequential symbolic gestures produce a symbolic exchange, as with gifts or favours. Here, the purpose is to build and maintain bonds of kinship amongst a community through never-ending cycles of tit for tat and quid pro quo emotional debt.

Symbolic exchange involves an amount of irrational risk that is integral to its operation, and as a consequence it exists outside the basic logic of capitalism (where two agents will only trade for the rational purpose of mutual, immediate and assessable gain). Through this type of trade, human interpersonal and social relationships are prioritised, while value is destroyed and profit thrown away. Symbolic exchange is therefore something like an anti-capitalist commerce.

Since the communal debt that accumulates through symbolic exchange is social, and not financial, it can never be paid off – because it can never be quantified. Costing up the goodwill of a neighbour is as absurd as putting an hourly rate on the love of a parent. Instead, this emotional debt passes back and forth around a community, creating societal interdependence and thus stability. In order to function, symbolic exchange also has to move back and forward across time, drawing past and future into the present. In very complex examples, emotional debts can lay dormant for generations before they are invoked and activated. This vision of time is circular, rolling in perpetual cycles such that death itself assumes an active role in the world of the living. As such, it stands in opposition to one of the most insidious fallacies of the Western worldview; that time, social and technological progress are linear. The importance of infinity in social debt is one reason Jean Baudrillard titled his theory *Symbolic Exchange and Death* (SAGE Press, 1993).

Like much of Baudrillard's work, the concept of symbolic exchange has been largely underappreciated in the decades since it was proposed. As a radical visionary, the French philosopher was in a sense too far ahead of his own times, and it is only in the last few years that his work has begun to appear as once again relevant (and even urgent). The value of Baudrillard's theory is both critical and propositional. It offers a structure for understanding the economy of affective labour, while also suggesting the possibility of a new type of multitudinous communism after (or outside) the nation state.

This small volume is published as a reflection on the 2015 Bold Tendencies exhibition, which took place from May 28 to September 27 within a disused multi-storey car park in Peckham, London. The exhibition included three site-specific public artworks: *Agora* by Richard Wentworth, *Possessed* by Metahaven and *Aspects of Change* by åyr. The latter two were commissioned by Attilia Fattori Franchini. As works within a curatorial framework they raised questions of civic space and participation, the remains of the commons, technology and affective relations, gentrification and urban renewal. Each of the artworks uses tangible material artefacts to explore these nebulous paradigmatic concerns, so the aspiration of this book was to find a way to construct a fluid editorial agenda around an exhibition that predates the book's conception. There is not a strong attempt to impose a reading onto these works, which each have their own interests and modes of expression. This book is, however, an effort to draw the works together through a common, productive lens.

In this light, symbolic exchange cuts across the three projects, and has obvious conceptual importance at a time when sharing means self-exploitation, and precarious labour dominates our lives. This book focuses on questions of wealth polarisation, urban renewal and real estate development, particularly as how they relate to the valuation of immaterial labour and the financialisation of identity politics – however it does so from the perspective of these phenomena as social power structures and moral assertions, not economic inevitabilities.

Although *Symbolic Exchange* adopts Baudrillard's framework for considering capital accumulation (both financial and social) in the urban realm, its existence as a response to singular, public, non-commercial artworks negates the accumulative cultural process. The lives of these artworks are grounded in our present condition and its linear future, not cyclical time – Baudrillard's death is absent from this exchange, and thus removed from the title.

Sharing is Caring
Metahaven (M) interviewed by Jack Self (JS)

JS
Symbolic Exchange and Death explores the life of icons when they become separated from any value assessment. In some respects, you could say it is concerned with how we assess the value of non-referential or immaterial forms. The reason we removed death from the title is because Baudrillard says that this form of exchange relies on a rupture in the distinction between life and death. It draws the deceased into the realm of the living to create cyclical time. But for contemporary capitalist society the exchange process is definitely linear. Its accumulation cannot incorporate death, or very possibly we live in a time that is already post-death. One of the scarves from your work Possessed contains a reference to Francis Fukuyama, who in turn references Nietzsche: *The End of History and the Last Man* – is the context for this work a post-death world?

M
We've been preparing a feature film, titled *Possessed,* for several years, and it is now in pre-production. This is probably the largest project we've ever done, something quite long-term. The way this all started was when we were giving a talk in 2014 which was called *Possessed By Us* and it was around the ways in which we have become addicted to each other through the interface of technology, and how we've become used to experiencing parts of

the other's presence or absence through such interfaces, we are 'possessed by us.' The talk then went into the work of cognitive scientist Douglas Hofstadter who has, based on personal experience, pieced together a working theory that proposes that we do not own our own selves but share them with others. The talk connected this with Snapchat with its ghost logo. As desire, anxiety, and other emotions are mediated through software platforms, we asked ourselves if there is a new form of belonging, new commonality, even a new communism, in that process? We decided we would develop this talk into some kind of screenplay.

In the film, a group of people live in a dysfunctional airport that has fallen prey to real estate speculation. When Bold Tendencies approached us, we thought we might produce some of the prototypes for the veils and outfits that are worn by this group or tribe, survey the possibilities and then actually testthe aesthetic. The feeling of post-death you just spoke about is present in the designs of some of the garments. We've been for a long time interested in the architecture of cloud computing precisely because this architecture was sold to us as a kind of ghost. And after we had been researching that for some time, and had been talking about how the cloud is physical (*Captives if the Cloud*), we also grew a bit more hesitant about approaches that try to explain the internet entirely out of its physical footprint. Indeed, all notions of the immateriality of the internet have been dismantled; there is no cloud but a massive 'accidental megastructure,' as Benjamin H. Bratton prefers to call it. Data is physical and its weight has an impact on the world. We became increasingly interested in how the internet transforms us emotionally, psychologically–how it traumatizes us, in a way. Brian Kuan Wood talked about this in his essay *Is it Love?,* coming from the perspective of love as a form of labor. An early version of his essay became the basis for the narration for our 2014 short film, *City Rising,* which featured models from Constant's *New Babylon.*

We started to become interested in sleep. Sleep, our last resort of time spent unproductively and offline, is accompanied by smartphones, tablets and laptops. We take these devices to our beds and sleep with them. And they are connections, people, desires, anxieties, work relationships, 'opportunities,' status updates, last seen, etc., transforming our minds. Toleep becomes an act of of resistance–as has been so effectively argued by Jonathan Crary in *24/7.* You could say that sleep is an invaded spacetime where we used to locate the core of the self–in its dreams. A century ago from now people slept a lot more, or perhaps, there was a more clear timespace associated with it. The smartphone has made the largest advance into this domain. The thing is that it is both a proxy for intimacy *and* for productive labor in the hypercompetitive sphere, where you have to be on high alert all the time to not miss opportunities. There's now a company that calls sleep 'fatigue management.'

We started thinking about how 'new communism' relates to sleep. We've built new networks and new affects that transcend the family, the city, and the nation-state. Most of these affects emerge around the admission of a shared desperation.

JS

I'm very interested by how immaterial or digital communication becomes manifest in space and time, something central to your work. Particularly, you present precariousness almost as a schizophrenic struggle. It is between boredom and romance, between extreme optimism and nihilism, and also between repetition and the cliché, against virtuosity and originality.

M

Boris Groys has said that when you become an activist or a 'political artist' (and maybe we should first agree that all art is political so there can't be 'political art') the first thing you would normally renounce is aesthetics, relating to Walter Benjamin's idea that fascism was signified by the aestheticisation of politics. Today however almost everything is subject to mediation, even and especially intimacies. The idea that aesthetics are working to the disadvantage of 'proper' politization needs to be abandoned in favor of a more open attitude to the ways in which both can coexist.

We have created some decidedly hysterical or ecstatic works. There is even a sense of desperation. On the other hand, we feel breathless, excited, curious. In art, and especially in design, there is this old dichotomy between essentialism and decoration. The two approaches both result in 'styles,' one that moves toward reduction (a stripping back) and the other toward ornament (a layering). Of course now we are at a moment when the mechanical processes and economies that historically led to this split no longer matter so much. In digital image-making standardisation is not at the level of mechanical or industrial fabrication (as in: a square block is cheaper to make than an ornate lion statue), but rather in the possibilities of software used to create the shape, to produce it, and platforms on which it is circulated. This doesn't say anything about the image itself but says something about circulation versus industrial production. The image can become a vehicle for all those desires, accumulative and multiple, and not singular or reduced. Images are becoming increasingly narrative, increasingly cinematic, in terms of a vision of the world and the power of what the image can do.

An emotional layering can be an expression of a drive towards the future. It is an approach that rejects reduction, and favors expansion.

JS
One thing that comes out of that is the role of aesthetics in political discourse. It's less and less common to see artists embracing so forcefully the re-appropriation of existing aesthetics. It creates in the work a level of tension and ambiguity as to whether the work is a proposition or a critique. It has both these kinds of qualities of the positive and the negative. For example, the snippets of conversation from Tinder that are portrayed on one of the scarves are totally clichéd

–this suggests a certain pessimism about love, and a kind of desperation to that conversation. On the other hand, this scarf's place in the project as a whole, which is a post-historical fashion collection, makes a clear positive and material proposition. Is this role of ambiguity key to the work?

M
We are interested in juxtaposing different value systems of imagery against each other within a single surface. If that's the feeling of tension you're describing that's very much intentional. The collision of these different symbolic languages can create a very different force... a different energy or meaning. It's very hard to talk about because it's a system of language that exists only in images. It can't be described easily in text, and it is present in almost every work we make.

JS
It's very powerful how even the title itself, Possessed, reflects a duality (not ambiguity) that is at once demonic and romantic. I wonder what this says about the possibility of positivity in the world.

M
The car park is a space that is very hard to predict, because it's open air. That's great, and very difficult. You think you know what everything will feel like, but it is changing all the time. It can be very cold, it can be really hot, the light is always changing. We tried to bring the installation to life, in response. We added brightly coloured

sand to some of the palettes, which blows and moves throughout the installation. We tried to use that kind of direct sense of the reality of being in that space and using the environment.

JS
You have highlighted the separation of content from its media, which was an idea also present in your previous works like *Can Jokes Bring Down Governments?* This permits variations of response, but not a fundamental challenge to the question. You can form infinite forms of content, but you can't restructure the platform used to create and disseminate the work: you can't rewrite the software, you can't create your own social media. The models of exchange of media and communication seem predetermined, so this is what I understood by the expression.

M
It brings to mind various signs that point in that direction, the fact that you can't challenge the question–you have to accept formats that are given to you by communicative capitalism. One point to make is that there is no predetermined political sign language, there are no fixed tools or symbols or icons. The process of politicisation of images occurs in such a way that signs that have an unrelated intent or content can acquire an extremely politicized meaning. The metaphor we used for this is to say 'there is no political cardboard.' When you go out and buy cardboard, for example at a hardware store, it has no predetermined use. At the moment of rupture, or at a tipping point, the cardboard can

become a sign of protest and become politicised. However, this idea of Lolcats and Rick Astley videos becoming viral weapons is increasingly eclipsed, not so much by governmental control of the internet as much as by the self-containment of platform culture where each has its own trending memes and distributive dynamics, and this has become accepted as a new form of informational privilege (enjoyed by the trending subject) rather than a sign of social change. The tagline 'within hours, so-and-so was trending on Twitter' has now become a mainstream way of demonstrating that something is newsworthy because it is popular. We met a filmmaker in Mexico City who is working with a Spanish migrant who has posted YouTube videos of himself that have accumulated tens of millions of views. When the guy was arrested by police, they realized that he was highly popular on the internet and they asked him to sing for them whilst in custody. Then cops started to make videos with their smartphones. That person now has a residency permit on the arbitrary basis of his online success, whereas there is at the same time an unprecedented crackdown on other undocumented migrants who have been trying to unionize and use other traditional political strategies for collectivization. We thought this was an interesting example because memes are increasingly treated as reasons to zero in on individuals instead of the cause that they represent. yber-anarchic sentiment that peaked a couple of years ago always was about cross-platform change and the open internet, and now we seem to be going through some kind of post-phase or hangover of that. The main focus of posting on platforms is the self. Many 'political' artists have become chroniclers of their egotastic fragmented autobiographies and seem unable to think or something else than the self. We've lost interest in the internet, in a way, we've lost interest in there being a network of networks and in that being a 'public space.' (quotation marks intentional). So a new and sneakier route leads through the various platforms that mediate the self.

JS
In the most recent figures from the Office for National Statistics (ONS) and Office of Fair Trading in Communations (OFCOM), it appears that 2014 was the first year in British history when media use outstripped the amount of time we spend sleeping. Although, it gets weirder; the average British person spends more than 14 hours per day using communication technology, yet they cram that into 8 hours 41 minutes. In other words, we're multitasking. That's 20 minutes more per day than we spend sleeping. 2014 was also the first year that the bed became the primary piece of furniture in the British home. It has become more used than the sofa, which also shows quite a fundamental shift in where that immaterial labour is occurring – imagining that social media is also a form of affective production for the platforms, Instagram, Facebook, and so on.

M
Yes.

JS
I want to ask about the platform for display of the textiles, which has been given a separate title *Grey Non-Market*. You've described it as a palette megastructure. Do you believe that within the current exploitative models of something like the sharing economy that there is a real possibility of communitarian exchange, which might be potentially non-commercial?

M
That's definitely something we thought about. Technically this installation was not a market; the pieces were not for sale. But the platform trade in emotions is also grey, in that it may sit within recognisable markets (like Tinder for example) but it also cannot be encompassed by them. Visually, the installation resorted to the aesthetic of street sellers to some extent, which is a non-permanent condition and which retains a feeling of temporality to it.

We wanted to avoid any interpretation of these garments as paintings or anything resembling the values that comes with exhibiting things on the wall. On the floor it seems more like a tapestry or even the display of wares by the street-seller. We wanted to play with an informality that can change the value of the artwork.

The grey market is a semi-legal, unregulated, form of exchange and therefore the particular bonds or relationships between agents are more important than when there is oversight by an authority or legislator.

With regards to the possibility for a nascent new communism, one of the driving factors behind the original *Possessed By Us* essay was that in fact maybe the way we feel about each other in terms of the relationships we pmay form is already far beyond any traditional structure that still existed. The way these relationships express themselves seems to be in duality between two people, but sometimes via these tools a kind of multitudinous communication arises; it doesn't run on a manifesto, but on asystemic power relational structure between users and the platform that structurates their interaction through its interface and holds their data.

JS
I want to pick up on one message from the veils. The textile that says 'The End of History and the Last Man,' is this a posthistorical fashion collection?

M
Yes. That would be a good motto for it. The reason that Fukuyama's book cover appears on the textile is that he was one of the main proponents of the end of oppositional politics, of the dialectical model where one power or one form of hegemony always has to face a counter-hegemony. In a sense, what we're doing now is that we live under a de facto single hegemony, but in that world we can't spiritually survive. We feel that we must build alternatives, that alternatives are needed and that we can't live in only one system. Maybe we need that sense of a collectively shared self.

Never At Home
åyr (å) Interviewed by Jack Self (JS)

JS
The project is called *Aspects of Change*, could you briefly give a description of the work and the space it occupies?

å
This work was a commission by Bold Tendencies, which for the last decade has organised annual exhibitions in a car park in south London. The project this year was curated by Attilia Fattori Franchini, who was interested in questions surrounding gentrification and mobility within the city, and how these were manifest in Peckham in particular. We immediately thought of working with images as the subject matter of the work, and with a particular image form, which is the 'render' as it appears within real estate websites or the communication of real estate agencies. We feel this type of image is a form of currency that is both virtual and real, and one that vastly affects how local urban dynamics function.

The way we work always addresses the context in which we find ourselves, and this particular site actually operates as a kind of machine for gentrification. What we wanted to do was discuss the image that comes out of this gentrification, and how that image can occupy more than a virtual space and begin to occupy physical space. We wanted to address the render, not just as an image or collection of pixels, but as an architectural element. From very early on we wanted to deal with the image as a wall, one that could divide the space.

We installed a series of six light boxes in the car park on the third floor. The space is exposed; outdoors, but covered. The images on the light boxes are full-size interiors, which introduced another kind of perspective or depth to the space. Our first response was to the architectural context of the car park itself, which involved the construction of partitions or walls to give a new spatial dimension to our intervention. This was also very much framed by Attilia's curatorial vision, that the works would address the car park as a building. At the same time, we wanted to deal with the larger cultural context of Peckham.

Peckham is one of the, let's say, 'up and coming' areas in London for the so-called creative class. Over the last five years there has been a rise in artists moving to Peckham, because it's close to a number of art schools and also because it's one of the areas that up until recently has been quite inexpensive to rent and live. Obviously this is now changing as a result of gentrification, and for every gallery that opens there is a developer around the corner trying to capitalise on the new population and energy it brings.

We had this sense that this car park is always in the developers' minds somehow as an oasis of culture. They frequently try to recreate the concept of the Peckham car park, which is that you bring in artists that start operating on a site that is not obviously useful. This generates interest, and then you develop it. Somehow we wanted to interject in that story, by bringing the violence of the future development into the present.

That brings us back to the title of the show, which is a paraphrase of an essay written by Ruth Glass called *The Aspect of Change*, which in fact coined the term 'gentrification.' This word was created specifically to refer to London at the end of the 1960s, which relates closely to our own intervention.

JS
To pick up on this question of gentrification, during the installation there was a lot of tension surrounding these questions of diversity, multiculturalism... how would you comment on the difference between gentrification and regeneration? The latter seems to have as its object the improvement of the standard of living for a local population, while the former seems really about displacement.

å
Initially, we didn't want to concentrate too heavily on gentrification, because the word can be seen as a cliché or even banal. But in a way the fact the word is almost dead offered it a new life. We didn't want to be seen as decrying or lamenting gentrification, because it's in the nature of urban renewal. This is especially true in a city like London, which has been in a state of constant change at least since the Great Fire of 1666. At the same time, there is one element that marks a big difference between then and today and that is that gentrification is now attached to speculation.

Over the last few decades there has been a massive increase in property speculation in London; it has coincided with the state progressively giving up its role in what could be called a positive gentrification, or perhaps regeneration. Whereas the state used to be responsible for the urban prosperity of its citizens, that project has now been handed to private developers.

As a word, regeneration has undergone a similar process to gentrification, in that it has become separated from its previous meaning until it becomes a quasi-apologetic term often used by the media to highlight a problem that we all know exists. The terms regeneration and gentrification once referred to distinct activities, but now their differences are largely meaningless. Re-labelling gentrification as regeneration is somehow trying to depict the city as an organism that is responsible for its own survival. Historically this isn't the case, as the governance of cities has always been conceived as the responsibility of the state. But when the state is weak, suddenly it is the role of the people to repair the tissue in this organic metaphor.

In this sense, what separates åyr from other artist groups or collectives operating from an architectural perspective, like Assemble, is that by making projects from very little they validate the idea that the market can be responsible for everything. Their work suggests that community work can be left to interested parties and artist collectives to the self-initiate. This paints community as representing only private agendas, which we think is deleterious to society.

JS
In your artist statement you referred to self-initiated community projects as a form of self-sabotage.

å
That includes both this form of collective art practice, as well as these kinds of 'project spaces' prevalent, for example, in Peckham. The concept of a project space is to act as an independent exhibition space for emerging or experimental artists. Those spaces try to have a role that is positive in trying to resist this process. But at the same time, it's clear they are integral to gentrification.

We had a public programme surrounding our own work, which involved working with several of the project spaces in the Peckham area. We invited them to the site, but they all had this negative reaction toward Bold Tendencies. They saw it as a programme that is pushing them out, but our question remains – how are these project spaces different? Aren't they also responsible for accelerating gentrification?

JS
Bold Tendencies and the project spaces use the same structure for quite different ends. They are both embedded in certain art communities, which might be more or less local; they are both engaging with a public audience, which again might be more or less local. You talk about the existence of the local and the authentic as potential conditions. In order for there to be a difference between project spaces and Bold Tendencies, doesn't that possibility need to be realised?

å

To respond to this question involves looking at what is now happening to the car park. There are proposals for redevelopment going in to the council, and the way the council is reacting to those proposals. Hannah Barry partnered with Second Home to transform the car park into a collection of affordable artist studios because that's what they felt was lacking in Peckham specifically and London generally. The proposal considered that what was 'authentic', and therefore in need of protection, was the artistic community.

The proposal was rejected because the council thought the artists were secondary to the real 'authentic' Afro-Caribbean population. That highlights the problem with the question of authenticity. It's always an instrumentalised concept of who was there first, and who has the right to be there. The obsession with authenticity distracts from the reality that there is no one really to blame for the fact there is no politics to the city, no new building, no new space. Everyone is being pushed out.

JS

The choice is either to leave or to share?

å

That's right. There is one small intervention called *Split Fear*, hidden at the edge of the space just as a momento mori would be in a renaissance painting. We collected letters from vintage stores in Shoreditch to compose the words split and fear, which is a riff on the 'split fare' command within the application Uber (to share the cost of a car ride with your peers). By reversing the letters we hoped to highlight this violent condition: if before we were splitting the proceeds of the welfare state, now we are sharing a common dread and anxiety about our lives...

JS
The project also deals with questions of temporary domesticity, or ephemerality in the domestic condition. The slogan for Airbnb–which I am obliged to say you are not now, nor ever have been in any way affiliated or endorsed–is 'belong anywhere.' Do you think belonging is in any case still possible today?

å
The question is not whether it is possible. The question is that on our side of the frontier, which divides the man with possibilities from the man with responsibilities, belonging is a condition that is forced upon us.

A couple of months after we did our first project [the *Airbnb Pavilion* at the 2014 Venice Biennale of Architecture] we began to address the concept of belonging nowhere. Paul Virilio describes the nomad as the one who is never at home, whereas the traveller is one who is at home anywhere. This entire structure relies on physical conceptions of the home.

JS
I want to return to the content of the images themselves. Is it fair to call the spaces you presented, these kinds of transient spaces, a form of home?

å

What is being depicted is an aspirational lifestyle that you find on platforms like Airbnb, but it's also some kind of portrait of the creative class and its relation to gentrification, which is a kind of mood. The affective forces that are manifest in these images enable the process of gentrification. This idea of homemaking, or making yourself at home, relies on your internal ideal projections onto a space. You must be able to project yourself, as someone, else into the space of the home.

There are six images, three of which are based on real artists' home–or the creative classes rather, since they are not all literally artists. One is the home of Cindy Sherman in the Hamptons. One is the home of the poet John Giorno in Soho, New York. One is the London home of Tom Ford. We took these spaces and we then elaborated upon them using a commercial rendering company. The other three are imagined as the typical, generic interiors of image-sharing sites like Pinterest. These are the domestic interior version of the Tomb of the Unknown Soldier. We used references from images that were as much monumental as they were common.

The artists' interiors are effectively self-portraits. We're interested in how interior decoration self-portraiture by the famous can also apply and be relevant to mainstream cultural norms (where people also intend their homes to be seen). The general populace now prepare the home for someone to see, it is the same process of self-portraiture present in Cindy

Sherman preparing the home for a magazine photographer.

JS
We've discussed previously the subjectivity of the artist and their role in this process of gentrification, and also an expanded definition of the artist as an entrepreneurial and autonomous form of labour. Is the artist today a general condition?

å
In this project we inhabit a ground that is both that of an art collective, so we are the same subject we are addressing, but at the same time our background is architecture–we are all architects–which is obviously entirely different and opposed. The architect considers ideas of community and master planning in completely different ways. Having one foot in both camps helped us define that subjectivity: we must be self-reflective from the point of view of what an architect thinks the artist might be.

The artist today is a heroic figure of self-realisation–who is herself to fullest, you could say–and who only reacts, or is reactive. The problems we encountered with the local project spaces concerned their conception of art as a reaction to whatever power is antagonising them. The notion of reaction is deeply embedded within the process of self-realisation, since one instinctively confronts only what is immediately threatening for survival.

JS
Critical art, which is today perhaps the dominant

form of art, aims to raise awareness in the viewer of a particular condition by capturing their attention. It is therefore premised on an idea of translation, education, representation and the pursuit of a didactic agenda (which may be softened, or blunted, by irony). However, critical art is a normative practice, it cannot fundamentally become positive. This could be contrasted against the role of the architect, which has historically always been embedded in a condition of design and proposition.

å
Yes, although we should clarify: we have no pedagogical intent with these images. They are not didactic, nor are they indexical. They do not even try to raise awareness in the viewer, nor do we expect or desire a certain response. They are violent depictions. We are not trying to 'make art' per se. We are trying to make images that embody and capture the tensions and violence of the context. The product of that attempt is the artwork.

JS
On this note, I want to bring up the 'sublet' programme, and particularly the project with the weaves.

å
What we did with the 'sublet' programme was to actively let go and become less controlling. When Attilia first commissioned us she spoke about Bold Tendencies as a piece of public art. It doesn't feel to us truly public. Most of the

people who experience the work are on their way to the bar and terrace. So finding ways to engage people who would not otherwise come to the car park was for us very important.

One side of the light boxes was opaque, so for the sublet programme we invited a number of organisations to introduce their own works to the space. The origin of calling it a 'sublet' was of course Airbnb, but in a broader sense, we were interested in what subletting means for local communities and for cities. It was also about giving up our own artistic agency. We worked with Schulden Programme, which is run by Jeremy Waterfield. This involved a number of site-specific additions to the images of the rooms. We also worked with a local school, and ran a project on the essence of home. They produced these really beautiful objects, not unlike tiny teacups – somehow a very British response. We hung them on the opaque faces of the light boxes. It was incredible to see what home really means to the children of this area, especially where you have, on the other side of the light box, a vision of reality that is so violent.

Another project was the two chandeliers designed by Ingo Maurer in the late 1990s, which are essentially appropriated design objects. The idea for the chandelier is that they are participatory design, and pertains to how relational aesthetics infiltrated the realm of design.

The chandelier comes as a bundle of steel rods and alligator clips with a bundle of paper that you as the owner are asked to customise. The assemblage of the lamp involves a certain degree of creativity and labour. Half of the pieces of paper come printed already, and half are unprinted. There is an element of curation of the existing statements, the text for which is a kind of global jargon of domestic welcomes. The user is required to participate in the design process. We adapted that process or concept of design by inviting Isaac Lock to write a series of Airbnb reviews. They are at a tangent between the fictional and the real.

We often use design objects in a completely pure form of appropriation; displacing an object outside of its context, but not intervening with them. This is because there is a specific design ideology present within these pieces that is powerful enough without being further modified.

These chandeliers are normally put inside a home, so to install them in a public place gives their participatory aspect new meaning. At first Isaac Lock's work was displayed. Subsequently to that, we replaced the writing with hair extensions that came from around the area. This played into the beautification of the lamp, but also referred to the beautification of the body, the area, and the city. This concept of improvement is the unifying theme of the exhibition.

There was at one moment a question as to whether putting hair extensions on the chandelier implicated a certain racial demographic. The shops in the area where we bought these extensions cater predominantly to an Afro-Caribbean community. In the end we used blond weaves to make sure the focus was on beautification, which is a universal construct, and to not foreground a racial discourse. The problematic was that because of the specificity of the context, it is doubtful whether simply making the weaves blonde has the power to ensure it remains a global statement. You can't ignore the reality, or the preconceptions that come with those objects.

However, this is not a project about identity politics, it is about domesticity, so we shouldn't focus too much on this one aspect.

JS
You described the idea of the image as a form of currency in circulation. The project resembles in many ways the hoardings that are erected around construction sites, which promise a certain vision of a completed project while the building itself is being built. For this simulation of desire, the image circulates in an economy almost independent of any reality. I wondered whether they are at all related to the literal or material nature of what they represent? Or, does the image exist in a domain that has no ties to physicality?

å
The images are technically executed in collaboration with a commercial rendering firm, which is another example of our willingness to relinquish autonomy over the artwork itself. We interacted with the render through the establishment of a basic framework and then guiding principles and references, much as a developer would do. On the other hand, this idea of the image being detached from the reality

is something the piece tries to supersede. The work refers to a particular pictorial trope, which is the trompe l'oeil. In fact, we are not talking about a representation, because this form is structural to the spaces within which they are embedded. There is a strong phenomenological dimension, but not only, as they have an architectural reality. They are not images conceived as an augmentation or afterthought, but integrally to the space. This is the same relationship rendered images have with their development. We cannot talk about two independent realms, in some ways.

In all our work we try to question whether it is possible for us to live in such poor material conditions–precarity, small apartments–just because we have such a wealth of images. Such a flow of images of domestic space act as a type of fantasy, but also hope, and allow you to visualise yourself somewhere else.

Can you be at home anywhere? These images give you the framework to allow you to inhabit spaces that you don't know. They are an aesthetic manual for feeling at home, which is the core of our exploration into the essence of taste.

The power of images in architecture comes at the same time and grows at the same rate as the process of transformation of the house into a financial asset, which is something we all know, but which is one of the main reasons we want to use renders is exactly that. The render as a tool becomes a hyperrealistic depiction of domesticity because it needs to depict both architectural space–its tectonic qualities–and its subjectivities–its lifestyles and objects.

As the finances underpinning the home become more immaterial, and more digital, so too do its images.

What happens is that when the home becomes an asset, there is no reason to inhabit it. Real estate is developed on a purely financial idea that bears no reality to the city.

[illegible] stic for many
[illegible] s self-ev [illegible]
[illegible]

Framing åyr's House of Terror
Federico Campagna

The apparent completeness of nature has always been a source of wonder, and for many throughout the centuries has served as self-evident proof of intelligent design behind creation. Even in the Ouroboros (the ancient symbol of a snake endlessly biting its own tale) the universe is depicted as a whole closed onto itself. Beyond mere self-sufficiency in terms of catering to one's own needs, closure is to be understood as the allegorical sign of metaphysical ripeness. Nothing that isn't complete can be perfect or, for that matter, real. Aristotle sums up this archetypal conception in his Physics:

> 'What has nothing outside it is complete and whole. For thus we define the whole–that from which nothing is wanting, as a whole man or a whole coffer. [...] On the other hand that from which something is absent and outside, however small that may be, is not 'all'. 'Whole' and 'complete' are either quite identical or closely akin. Nothing is perfect (*teleion*) which has no end (*telos*); and the end is a limit.' (1)

This explains the profound suspicion shared by prophets and philosophers alike towards the problem of the image. The image appears to be the weak link of reality: that which is never closed onto itself. An image always seems to cry out for an object of representation, for the process of representation itself–as well as for a creator and for a final viewer.

In a sense, the problem of the image is the same as the problem of knowledge. Like the image, knowledge also appears incomplete in itself, as it is perennially looking for its own object, for its own subject, and for the very process that animates it. The task of tying together these three ends–the knower, the known and the knowledge itself–had occupied generations of philosophers and mystics until the great 12th-century Andalusian thinker Ibn Arabi put an end to the inquiry. According to Ibn Arabi, the coincidence of these three elements is both the sign and the essence of the achievement of the pinnacle of understanding and contemplation.

When applied to the question of the image, however, this perfect coincidence appears as impossible. Even if it we were to assume the identity between the creator of an image, the object of its representation and the act of representation itself–parallel to Ibn Arabi's vision–it would still remain lacking its fourth constitutive element: the final viewer. The viewer enters the equation of wholeness and shatters it, making resolution impossible, opening within it a gaping abyss.

The abyss of the image–that same metaphysical abyss that had bothered thinkers like Parmenides and Plato–remained at the heart of aesthetic thinking well beyond the end of antiquity. Of all the centres of engagement with this problem, it was perhaps the Byzantine Orthodox church from which a possible solution to this enigma emerged. According to

Byzantine Orthodox iconography, the task of the icon painter is not merely the representation of an object, but rather the theurgic process of literally bringing the object of the painting (Christ, the Virgin, the Saints, etc) into the world through the image. An icon is not just a painting: it hosts the very presence of the divine entity whose image it contains. According to the Russian philosopher Pavel Florensky, no one less than a saint would be able to turn raw matter into a suitable host for the divine, and nothing but this very task has to be understood as the duty of an icon painter. For Florensky, figures like St. Andrei Rublev, who was able to master this necessary double perfection as a saint and as an artist, are able simply through their painting to prove the very existence of the divine. Says Florensky, with lapidary brevity: 'There exists the icon of the Trinity by St. Andrei Rublev; therefore God exists.'

Yet, even this doesn't resolve the problem of the fourth side of the equation: the final viewer. How can the viewer – in the context of Orthodox Christianity, the mere believer – be brought back in perfect unity with the rest of the accomplished image? This seemingly impossible task is entrusted by Byzantine Orthodox iconology to the most miraculous of substances: gold, as it embodies the absolute 'yes' that God bestowed upon reality, thus making it real and whole. In an icon, the golden background doesn't only confirm the reality of the images that it surrounds, but it overspills outside the painting, towards the viewer. The viewer him/herself is touched by the light of gold, and is made to be again part of that same state of shared unity, wholeness and reality that is enjoyed by the image. The viewer is literally 'blessed' by the painting. The equation is closed.

And yet, somehow the traditional values of Byzantine Orthodox iconology are at the greatest possible distance from our contemporary world. In particular the idea of closure, of wholeness, and of the unity of reality appears to have completely vanished from our cultural horizon. At the end of the 19th century Paul Bourget defined 'decadence' as the process of dissolution of a unity, in which the parts leave the whole and take it over as an irresolvable multitude. Ever since, the problem of unity has progressively exited the range of our metaphysical and cultural concerns. After the combined triumph of decadence and nihilism, not only has the 'whole' ceased to exist even as a possibility, but the very concept of unity has undergone a fundamental crisis. Unity appears to be impossible both at a universal, macrocosmic level, and at the level of the tiniest microcosm, including the supposed wholeness of the individual subject him/herself. Not only has the whole been shattered, but so has each of its parts. The supposed reality of everything and anything has been thrown into question, and finally decreed to be false. Nothing is a unified whole in itself, nothing is real in itself, nothing is ever 'in itself'.

With the revolution brought by Nietzsche to Western philosophy, the very possibility of 'truth' in reality has been discarded as a perilous illusion: all that exists in the world is just an endless production of appearances, emerging out of the indomitable 'will to power' that animates each aspect of reality, spinning around itself as its own eternal return. Only images are real, and yet they are not real... They no longer represent anything, both because there is nothing left to represent, and because they are merely the emanation of will to power–the creative principle at the heart of reality. Perhaps paradoxically, the chimera of wholeness and unity–of the object, creator, viewer and process of the image–returns here, but only as a perpetually recurring instability. Thus transformed, the world becomes a desert of extinguished ashes–as in the exasperated and ultimately bloodless aestheticism of Gabriele D'Annunzio's late work *Il Fuoco*–that escapes the human ability to inhabit it. The only possible dweller of this new land is a new breed of human, the 'superman'.

The question of inhabiting is central here, both to the problem of the image after the final crisis of metaphysics, and to the work of åyr's *Aspects of Change* displayed at Bold Tendencies 2015.

Since the dawn of time, and according to the law of analogy, the microcosm of the house has been considered as a mirror of the macrocosm of the universe at large–of which it shares the same principles, laws, and problems. This correspondence is particularly visible in the traditional structure of the house, which, according to the Romanian historian of religion Mircea Eliade, is strictly regulated so as to display perfect adherence to the supposed structure of the cosmos. Still today, despite the storm of decadence, nihilism and capitalist secularisation of the last few centuries, this affinity between the house and the cosmos remains standing–perhaps necessarily, as a sort of inescapable archetypal connection.

In this sense, we could interpret the images used by åyr to describe the state of contemporary home-making as referring not only to the process of making-a-home, but also to that, more general, of making-a-world–or, in other words, of 'reality engineering'.

Once again, the fundamental question of the image returns in reference to åyr's work. Who created these images of world-making? What exactly do they depict? Who are they for? And, how do they represent their object? Already troubled by the constitutive openness of the status of the image, this equation here remains doubly unresolved, as it finds its own reflection in the double produced by irony. If they are to be understood as ironic images, they must be meant as the inquisitive mirror of some other, pre-existing images. Indeed, at first glance, åyr's works refer to pre-existing images from catalogue-like, interior design representations of a home–of which åyr replicates not only the actual likeness but also the essential internal motion. By inserting the original image inside itself in an endless loop, the original catalogue-like image of a home (and thus, archetypically, of the world) turns out to be a representation only of itself.

But this is just the most apparent aspect of åyr's work. In fact, the series of pictures doesn't merely refer to catalogue-like images in a loop. Rather, the object of each of åyr's images is the very act and process of self-replication, unfolding as an internal loop in which each circulation acts as a frame to each further inner reflection, *ad infinitum*. The content and variety of the image as such is here largely irrelevant, since the 'thing' that is depicted in each work is always the same: the infinite series of looping frames.

Thus, we can read this series of images produced by åyr as referring to contemporary interior design and neoliberal domesticity only in the most metaphysical sense. As if it was the embodiment of a nightmarish version of Nietzsche's 'eternal return', the home-world presented by åyr is essentially a frame that remains indifferent to its content–as long as this content can act in turn as a further frame, and so on, down to the infinitesimal level of molecular and atomic framing.

åyr's essential depiction of the contemporary home-world is not far from our everyday experience of it: finally devoid of sense or of any intrinsic meaning, the gaping abyss of reality produces a feeling of displacement so great that we must resort to any extreme just to keep hold of it. Damming the boundless abyss of nihilistic reality becomes a tacit yet powerful motivation at the heart of our relationship with our own individual and social life: so not to fully lose ourselves in reality, we must implement something that frames our experience of it.

Having already lost all faith in traditional methods of definition of limits–such as, for example, those that invoked 'essential' or 'natural' limits–we are now seeking just any frame, however arbitrary. Indeed, we prefer frames as blatantly arbitrary and as explicitly meaningless as possible: having grown suspicious of old forms of ideology and faith, we want to do without any relics of our traditional forms of framing as well. Our new frames, our new structures of existence, must be as bare and depthless, as invisible and all-encompassing as possible. The act of framing thus descends to the stage of a pathological reflex, an obsessive and compulsive attempt at securing our own presence in the world (and the presence of reality as such) through the most basic of methods: identity as incarceration, philosophy as pure policing, and so on. But this time, differently from the troubling age of metaphysics that we have left behind, we are doing without understanding justice, good and beauty as attempts to ennoble our pathological action.

At the same time, irony itself also functions as a frame–possibly, the largest and sturdiest of all. Just like the framing loops inside åyr's work (and perhaps, at the core of åyr's work itself) ironic criticism is a last ditch attempt at bringing reality back under control, while at the same time being unable to endow it with a form. Irony and criticism, muck like Nietzsche's *ressentiment*, is the ultimate form of post-ideological policing: pure *pouvoir* (power as domination and control) without *puissance* (power as creative praxis). In this sense, we can read ironic criticism as constitutively organic and instrumental to the same process that it wishes to critically and ironically attack.

Martin Heidegger used this same word, 'framing' (*Gestell*) to address the process of crystallisation of Being into the specific form of being, which he sees as the essence of metaphysics and the cause of the regrettable process of 'forgetting Being' which characterises Western philosophy. Trapped within a frame, Being ceases to reveal itself, its voice fades, and it ultimately appears to desiccate into mere beings – ready to be re-employed in the service of industrial production. The prime example of this nefarious framing process is, according to Heidegger, the current regime of 'Technic' (*Technik*). Technic is the supreme and final triumph of that essential Western mistake that is the attempt to 'conquer' reality rather than opening our 'ear' to it. Framing is thus fundamental to our constant attempt at reducing reality to a set of available resources, devoid of any profound internal specificity.

In this particular case we are discussing home-making and the issue of inhabiting a home-world. Accordingly, the reduction of reality to a 'stockpiling of standing reserves' (as per Heidegger's definition of Technic's outcome) goes hand in hand with the transformation of the house into a factory environment – one set up to reproduce exactly that same 'technical' relationship with reality that aims at reality's degradation and domination. But whose dominion is this? The process of framing doesn't spare the individual human, especially after the so-called Postfordist turn, founded on a further enslavement of human thoughts, emotions and bodies into the framing process. So this can't be the dominion of the individual human over reality. Is there perhaps a super-human or non-human force at work here? Almost, though not quite. Similarly to the way in which, according to Heidegger, the forms of remembering and forgetting of Being are historically defined (as in, they take on the character of each specific historical age), so the force propelling such forgetting (or framing) varies with each historical age. In this specific historical age, our age, this force is that of fear–or, better, terror.

Unlike panic, which makes its victims run amok frantically, terror produces a state of paralysed turmoil: a gaping mouth, eyes wide open, motionless limbs, fast-beating heart. Terror is a force that struggles to overcome itself, by grasping to hold onto anything in sight (irrespective of it being fantastic or real). Terror cries out for a frame to pull itself outside of itself.

The house-world of terror is thus one that loudly declares–shouts–its being a home, while simultaneously being fully aware of its uninhabitability. The house of terror is a circular prison, where all doors are open onto each other, and none towards an outside. Sunk in terror, as embodied by Technic's triumph, our forgetting of being is complete: nothing remains but the name of things, the image of their image, automatically produced as if by a hand struck by terror itself.

Even within the house-world of terror, as we experience it daily, another type of space remains possible. It is that 'wilderness' (*wildnis*) sought by the German thinker Ernst Junger, which still lies somewhere near us (perhaps, as we would claim, inside us), however invisible.

In his 1977 novel *Eumeswil*, Junger pictured this space as a bunker secretly built by the protagonist in the midst of a looming crisis that is soon to sweep over the libertarian dictatorship of the city of Eumeswil. It is perhaps at this point, where the bunker emerges from the shrubs that hide it, and its windows open over the beach, that our new work to attempt a recomposition of the image–of our own life, as it takes place in the home–world–can finally begin again.

But first, as we attempt to find an oasis from which to restart, we must be able to retain the secret of its location. In order to be able to find again the bliss of the composed icon, we must pass through the silent process of iconoclasm, as it was first historically understood.

(1) Aristotle, Physics, III, 6, 207 a 7–15
(author's translation)

Imaginative Duty
Suzanne Hall (SH) interviewed
by Shumi Bose (SB)

SH
I think if architecture is to be relevant in the twenty first century, it has to engage with the structures of power.

SB
On discussing his piece Agora, Richard Wentworth and I ended up talking about implications–about being implicated in the swirling structures of class and power politics, which I thought was as clear a descriptions of an artist's own work as I've ever heard. You've looked at Peckham in some detail; tell me some stories. What made you want to study it?

SH
Well I lived nearby, for a start. Because so my much of my work concerns ethnography, it is important for me to be able to engage with places quite directly, rather than be a visitor to them. My first work was on Walworth Road, which was much more about quiet interiors. Peckham is much more in your face, in an incredible way–I mean, in the true sense of the word, it is *vital*. I have never felt more affirmed as a newcomer to London as I am when I'm standing on Rye Lane or when I'm standing on the top floor of the Peckham Library at four in the afternoon, when the place is absolutely heaving. So I guess it was a sensuous response to a place, before it was a political one–that there was a palpable vitality.

SB
Is that becoming a more rarified experience in London?

SH
I think it's an unusual experience. What is also affirming is that it is not an experience that has been created by some kind of professional expertise. You could go to the British Museum and it would also be heaving and vital, but it's a highly specific, curated experience–and as a result, ends up being a middle-class experience. You go with a consciousness of being a museum-goer. [...]

I went to the car park to Frank's Bar, on the rooftop, before I met Hannah. To be honest I found it a very dislodging experience. I found it highly curated, profoundly middle class–and almost perversely detached from the street, almost similar to my experience of growing up in South Africa, where you have got a white class world cheek-by-jowl with a more mixed world, and they don't in any way overlap. So I was absolutely astounded.

But then I had another dislodgement when I met Hannah and went to Bold Tendencies. And I was astounded again, because here is clearly a highly imaginative, highly courageous individual who takes all sorts of risks. And so I wonder, what is it about these profound creativities that sit alongside each other, that of the art world and of the street outside, but they don't interact. They are, literally, parallel forms of high-level imagination.

SB
That they don't explicitly intersect, though – is that necessarily a problem?

SH
I think it is. I actually do think it is. I think first of all, there is the difference between making artwork in a studio or in a gallery... and making work in a city that is changing in all sorts of important ways. If you choose to go to Peckham, somewhere on the outskirts that's simply cheap, rather than a gallery in Soho that attracts the high-flying buyers, if you're making that conscious choice to be somewhere else, then there is a responsibility to go beyond the fact that it's simply cheap. And I don't mean responsibility as some sort of moral duty. I mean it as an imaginative duty.

Maybe the art gallery remains fairly contained... But the minute you begin to do a public project or a public initiative where you promote some kind of exchange, I think it then becomes incumbent to question why does this exchange always take place over a cocktail, a cappuccino, or other highly curated forms of middle-class-dom?

SB
Perhaps there is a sort of trickle-down benefit assumed, that it will come down to the street.

SH
Which it doesn't. And I think there's a kind of violence to that. When I first went up to the roof, I was aware that I had to go through two security

points. This makes me very aware there are a whole lot of young black kids in Peckham who are never going to go up there. And I think that's a problem.

These kinds of dislodgements, while both creative, do procure a kind of violence. And I think it's the same kind of violence then when the Council comes in and doesn't recognise as having value, and ultimately doesn't recognise the car park as having value, as it turns out. If these kinds of energies had been more aligned, they might have been able to put up a better fight against what is happening.

SB
It becomes about porosity of access–an economic and cultural porosity rather than, or as well as a physical one. And those are the barriers to cross.

SH
There are examples of this. Hannah Jones, who runs the Peckham Chamber Orchestra, did something remarkably interesting. She looked at the Peckham Liberal Club, which is something like a hangover from the old working mens' club. It's essentially white, working class people over sixty who occupy the space, and they are short of money. Hannah spent a lot of time hanging out, drinking with them, so there was a socialising aspect, and finally thought if she was going to do a music venture in Peckham, this was the place. By having her music venture in the space, she cross-subsidises some of the other activities. So there is

a conversation, a dialogue, without this moral undertone of having an obligation or integration. There's mutual benefit, and it's done with ease and a kind of sensuality, I guess. So again that comes back to affordability of space, people being able to hang out in an easy way, and then something imaginative that seems to spark out of that overlap.

SB
How robust do you think Peckham really is? Sometimes you wonder where somewhere will be in two or three years' time...

SH
Hmm. Eight or ten years ago–before the 2008 crash–I would have put my head on a block to say that certainly Peckham, but possibly somewhere like Walworth Road too, would be reasonably safeguarded by virtue of its social housing estates: about three quarters of the populations who support those worlds, living in social housing. But that's the thing that is being wiped out of the equation. The minute you displace the residents, the social life, the public life becomes volatile.

I just assumed that public housing was sacrosanct, and I always thought that was one of the most astounding aspects of London, that you could have this proximity of public housing and other kinds of important opportunities. But in that sense London has become an incredibly hostile terrain. Because displacement has become *de rigeur*.

SB
Funnily, Richard was recollecting his time living off Walworth Road, watching the Heygate Estate as it was being built. Massive change was taking place, yet not in the same way. When were you researching there? What were you doing?

SH
We started in 2012, quite intuitively, with a group of students who were thinking about Peckham. The first thing we did was a very basic face-to-face survey of shops, where you try to get an interview with every proprietor. In the first round of that survey, two things stood out. One was that there were over 22 different countries of origin – and un-like countries of origin being cheek-by-jowl, so you'd have someone from Ghana sharing a shop with someone from Pakistan, next to someone from Malawi. Not even regional or cultural proximities. This is not the kind of Brixton Market, predominantly Afro-Caribbean; it's not Brick Lane. That was interesting in itself: is there a different kind of vitality that begins to arise, when very diverse populations from across the planet are co-proximate?

The thing that really blew us away though – and which was probably the over-riding story of Peckham – was the way that a huge proportion of the retail spaces were subdivided into little shops. That was driven by the reality that rents in Peckham were beginning to rise; in order to attend to the impact of the crisis, people started to subdivide their shops. But all sorts of interesting creativities emerge.

Really astutely, the space was divided not only in terms of space, but also through a variety of tenancies. So for example, if you're a young mum who can only work two days a week doing people's hair, that opportunity becomes available. And then these economies are organised spatially: the mobile phone guys, at the front of the shop, pay the highest rents, because they are in direct contact with the street. These guys are highly educated; they usually have or are doing postgraduate degrees, they've worked in computer science, they are manipulating software packages. The questions that arise are to do with the kinds of civility you might need when you share a space every day, and you've got to decide on things like who locks up at night, how you share a toilet. How it is that the guy handling thousands of pounds in money remittances and overseas transfers never gets hit?

By subdividing and making space affordable for an array of people, they allowing for all these adjacencies. Then there are all these bigger agreements of how do you all live side by side, every day. And it's a very pragmatic sense of agreement. Unlike this state-speak of the ideology of cohesion and integration, this is the pragmatic reasoning of how can we make business and how can we live comfortably together. But it gets very sophisticated. There is this incredible economic performance: Rye Lane provides more jobs that Westfield Stratford, for instance.

It's this kind of urbanism of the kind that Suketu Mehta wrote about, in The Guardian a few days ago, looking people who are renting a bed for eight hours at a time. (1) At that end, it's this highly exploitative land market. At this end, it is attending to the rise in the prices of the land market but it happens to work very well.

SB
In a very agile way.

SH
It's very agile. And it's unusual because actually our planning by-laws are fairly permissive in this respect, and the relationship between landowners and tenants are fairly permissive. At that point of our research, we decided that we needed a different vocabulary because what we were saying wasn't necessarily being heard. From that stage onwards, we always did these comparisons: here's a Westfield, you know it well. It has this kind of vocabulary that you know, and here is how Rye Lane speaks to it in the same terms.

SB
And did that get any further?

SH
No... No, it didn't. One employee said, you're showing us a city that is changing within the course of 24 hours, but our planning habits take at least five or ten years to change–what are we meant to do with this? And that is a real issue: if we're talking about strategic architecture, critical architecture, or purposeful design in the twenty first century, one of those things is to recognise that we need some form of mediation between large and small forces, whether

it's a version of providing a £100 rent, or a traders' association model, or this thing that allows a planner to engage with this 24 hour city. What constitutes this mediation? We've got to get a lot sharper at comprehending that. I think there is this ludicrous division between bottom-up and top-down, and it's not about that; it's about how you design relationships that allow people to have purposeful conversations.

SB
Coming back to the car park, as a place that allows people to have conversations–what do you think of it as a building?

SH
It's a funny building; I've always inhabited the front part, the Peckhamplex cinema. The car park is already tucked away and has this sort of secretive approach, which I think is probably interesting. It is something that is lifted from the ground. But the model of the Peckham Library just down the road is also lifted from the ground, and that gives it a phenomenal energy. We always speak of porosity as if it's a physical thing, or as if it's mixed-use, when actually the most powerful thing you could do is give that economic porosity. Because that's ultimately saying to someone, okay you're safe here for a while, without experiencing the threat of feeling dislodged.

(1) Suketu Mehta, 'Beyond the maximum: cities may be booming but who is invited to the party?' Guardian Cities, 30 November 2015 (online, last accessed 20.12.2015)

How we are Implicated
Richard Wentworth (RW) interviewed by Shumi Bose (SB)

SB
Let's talk about how the artwork on Bold Tendencies came about.

RW
I sent you two drawings, like this *[doodles a line of overlapping loops on the table mat]*

SB
They were lovely, but I don't know if the squiggle came first or the box-forms that they were folded into.

RW
That's exactly the point. Yes, my coffee! So, foreplay is still the funniest part of the art process. I don't really know Hannah. I understand exactly who she is and why we need people like her: we need a lot more people who are dis-conventional. I very much like the fact that she doesn't come from the subject, the art world. Gold dust! She wrote a really Hannah-ish email saying, 'I don't know what you know about Bold Tendencies...' To which the answer was 'Nothing', because you know, it's miles away! I don't have that sort of amusing time anymore, I don't even go to Shoreditch...

I actually know very well where it is, and it's probably best to tell this story as a dark thing. In the late sixties, I lived off the New Kent Road. I watched the clearance of the entire Heygate site, what streets went missing–there are streets under the Heygate, it was right outside my window. And then I watched it being built, and I watched the Aylesbury Estate happen; I had quite a powerful sense of Westminster to Camberwell. During that time, I got, more or less by accident, this building on the side of Southwark Park called Dilston Grove, a 1911 concrete church. When I say 'got it', people didn't speak about property; you looked for a studio. So in that studio was my best friend, who worked for Sottsass; an incredibly good artist called Carl Plackman, enormously influential–both of whom are dead, so I'm the last surviving man from that studio–my wife Jane, who was somebody else's wife; and her partnerships which were textiles and rag-trade. I now realise what a modern studio that was: someone coming from design, Carl who came from Giacometti, me, Jane and these partners. This was 1969 to 1978–I was teaching at Goldsmiths at that time, too.

But that means that before anyone really knew about Peckham or Camberwell or any of these places–I'm exaggerating but you know–I had been there. And the reason I've taken time to tell you, is because that is how Antony Gormley went to Peckham, that's why Antony went to live in Camberwell through that direct line through Charles and me...

SB
And so you sort of cracked into South London, do you think?

RW
Well, we've all got stories about where we live, but they've become unremarkable. Black and white A-to-Z, and a bad photocopy, a telephone number written down wrongly: that's how London used to work. Until 1995, or '97–until Blair, really. I think it's the Blair-digital axis that turned everything. So, and this will accelerate: we were immature; we had affairs; we weren't very badly behaved because actually no one was, except a very few; we bought tickets to see David Bowie and we would go; we built sets for Roxy Music in that studio.

SB
Did you have some sense of being pioneers?

RW
No. I mean, I was there but... The public record should be something to delight in, not this arrangement of Swarovski diamonds. It has probably always been mythology but I'm on some sort of moral... Anyway, late seventies; life proceeds: marriages split up; Jane and I get together; I start doing group therapy; my son Joe is born in 1980; Felix is born at 1982 and the week that Felix is born, Charles kills himself on the railway at Peckham.

SB
[I'm sorry, at–]

RW
Yes, so really I had sort of left South London behind–not that one ever calls it South London,

the Elephant is the centre of London. But it was totally off my menu. Even being in a car at Walworth Road would make me feel lachrymose. So when Hannah asked me, I thought this is weird. Do I want to go back there? Who am I?

It does mean that I have a very intense sense of what that place was. We can now see that we were students in the years after the war, in a London that was–even though Jane was a student in 1962, I was a student in 1965–still gripping the table post-war. What I mean is that the physical fabric of London was incredibly dirty, very cold, very wet, very damp. Everything was putrefying, with little bright spots: sex, short skirts, Mary Quant, Foale and Tuffin, and Carnaby Street. But it was a little scratch.

The way we were living was still linoleum, hall runners, the smell of cat's piss and old people, bad plumbing. No car regulation, no MOT, drink as much as you like, no parking charges–my second term at the Royal College, 1967, was when they put parking meters around the Albert Hall. Before that, you could park up my uncle's Renault outside the Royal College, and just leave it! That's what we don't talk about, when we say the fabric of the city.. So we were naive, and socially not as mixed as we think we were, but we were mixed. We talked in what I call the Commonwealth space, but it's one where I understood how I was implicated. And what I was always angry about is why don't people talk about how we are implicated.

But I also know what Heseltine and Thatcher and so on were doing, I get the desperation.

There was no Chinese money. You know I met Kissinger and he asked me about her? *[terrible impression of Kissinger]* 'Tell me about Mrs Thatcher, what is your view?' I gave him the Harold McMillan view, which is that she sold the family silver. But that's because I'm from a class that thinks it's got family silver!

SB
Does Southwark Council's car park count as the family silver?

RW
Well.. to go to the end and come back again: the boroughs that we talk about were invented in 1965. The GLC is invented in the Sixties, after the LCC. Inhabitants of the city were more or less in flight–the predominant card signs in the tube was 'A Government Agency to help you leave London', absolutely constant throughout the 1960s and 1970s.. Because London was in managed decline, and there was no value given to the middle class. [...]

Anyway, so Hannah intrigues me, because [...] I spend a lot of time thinking about what happens to youthful intelligence in my culture. In the same way as I say publicly, I don't know anyone in the political classes. They are nowhere near any of this. But I think this thing about the constituents of this class, who they all are–the trouble is you're very good at getting me to talk about it. Our whole conversation has sort of been about structures, but it's been about the unaccountability of these structures, there are these other forces.

SB
But getting back to this. *[tapping the doodle on the table mat]*

RW
I've done it, I've already done it *[uses an almost-exhausted pen to draw another looping, overlapping doodle]* So when a pen doesn't work, and you go like this.. that purposeful yet purposeless scribble. What you do is that you proceed but the line is going backwards. In order for the whole thing to proceed, it has to go backwards.

SB
Like a blanket stitch...

RW
Hm? That's interesting, it is like a blanket stitch but I heard Mandelbrot. If it's not in Einstein, it's got to be in brain science, it's got to be in physics and fractals somewhere. That's what our lives are: we're mostly going backwards, and we repeat ourselves. It's a form that interests me. So Hannah says come to the roof. We're standing on the roof, striding around the top of the car park. Which is of course very unusual, and I'd never been there. All I can think is that we're on a balcony; this must be in a history painting, but it is a public balcony. We're in a strange, compellingly safe place... You don't really understand why you feel okay up there, you feel like the king of the castle and it hasn't got any evident status. And she was saying, I know you could do something here. There was

a lot of clunky discussion around being an artist who likes architecture. Of course, what happens to artists is that any time you do a show, you're standing in ghosts.

SB
Had you thought about it being seen from above? One of the lovely moments was when it appeared on Google Maps.

RW
The answer is no. I thought of two things, one was how to find a form that was convincing, that was something you would almost take for granted. It had to feel inevitable and it had to implicate you. I had also started drawing and folding the drawing up. It was fun realising that the word 'to implicate' is also related to folding.

I knew it had to deal with optics and surface; you adjust your position to it. I just knew that if I could get that to work, and if you could be standing snared, and everyone else would be snared as well, then you could make an urban metaphor.

But it was never an illustration. I would hate to make work which started out with these kinds of conceits and then illustrated the point, but I recognise that anybody who makes it onto that roof is 'implicated' and of course that's what the city tells us again and again. I like the idea that somebody could be drunk there, and notice that the form is similar and different in every direction. I'm a bit passionate about desire lines and how paths get made such that large parts of London are evidently described by a mixture of cattle movements and property rights–which is not a bad metaphor for how we move along pavements, cross roads on the oblique and generally 'find our way'. The Google picture somehow imparts exactly those energies, in the same way that you can see the way that a path across some crappy public space dips to the left or the right, because there's a tree nearby.

The way we worked out how to do it was pretty smart, I think... and of course, no one ever saw it from above so when we did see it, we thought, not bad! We made hardboard templates–well, first we worked out the scale of it with hosepipe, and realised that this can't be a 30mm strip. It's a strip, not a line but it's not quite a path. Although children use it as a path, which is lovely to see. It's like standing in a puddle and somebody saying have you noticed what you're standing on.

The great thrill (and reward) with the Google moment came when suddenly you could see it as a totality, from a point of view that is profoundly conceptual. Yes, I was there when they landed on the moon and looked back and spoke with American awe...

SB
You called it Agora, which suggests the market and things to do with publicness. You know, there are so many artworks with that name! What did you mean?

RW
I meant my classical education! *[laughs]* All I

really knew was that I needed to do something that was ensnaring and insinuating but without any meanness - a kind of surreptitious act which the humblest footfall would find itself engaged in. I realised that the way it is made and its scale is almost as if it were 'carpeted' for a 'public'. Hard grade asphalt properly laid has that allure.

Concourse or Agora were the two names we thought about. No, I meant to use Agora as a much better term than forum – one where your moral and political responsibility is implicated, even if you don't know that it is.

Do Algorithms have Epiphanies?
Tamar Shafrir

In the final chapter of *A Portrait of the Artist as a Young Man*, Stephen Dedalus faces a basic problem. As he expounds his aesthetic theory in dialogue with his friend Cranly, he asks how can beauty be defined if it varies from one viewer to another? He has two possible responses. The first is that, as in the adaptations of human beings to varying climates and ecosystems, beauty constitutes a specific set of standards (in his example, those of the ideal woman) that supports the continuation of the species in each territory. Dedalus finds this idea rather limiting, but takes more hope from his second hypothesis, in which beauty's constitutive qualities–wholeness, harmony, and radiance–transcend man's animalistic and tribal nature;(1) in which 'the WHATNESS of a thing' passes from the mind of the creator into a relationship with the other.

Intriguingly, James Joyce develops this passage differently in *Stephen Hero*, the literary precursor written a decade before the publication of *Portrait*. There, rather than raising the loaded question of embodied female beauty (particularly as a man in love), Stephen describes culture as a noisy thicket surrounding the pure concept of beauty:

> No aesthetic theory...is of any value that investigates with the aid of the lantern of tradition. What we symbolise in black the Chinaman may symbolise in yellow: each

has his own tradition. Greek beauty laughs at Coptic beauty and the American Indian derides them both. It is almost impossible to reconcile all tradition whereas it is by no means impossible to find the justification of every form of beauty which has ever been adored on the earth by an examination into the mechanism of aesthetic apprehension, whether it be dressed in red, white, yellow or black...This is the moment which I call epiphany.

Stephen's approach is relevant not only because it asks us to think about where beauty resides, but also because its reference to 'every form of beauty which has ever been adored on the earth' expands the territory of beauty to a seamless and infinitely scalable field. His understanding of beauty need not be (and in fact cannot be) hierarchical, but instead becomes shorthand for the aesthetic encounter as a way of confronting reality in general, or at least its visual counterpart. (2) Therefore, the main questions remain: if we take the 'whatness' as the content or currency of the aesthetic encounter and the epiphany as its medium, then what is their relationship to reality? How is that reality altered by the encounter? And does the participation of new forms of intelligence, specifically the algorithmic, complicate not only the encounter but also reality itself?

It would be easy, of course, to say that reality exists only within the epiphany; that it is endlessly recreated in each encounter; and that the multiplication of realities emerging from aesthetic encounters is governed by the same economy as that which exists in any other realm of technologically-mediated human activity. But the aforementioned 'whatness' presents a thorny contradiction: though we might acknowledge two simultaneous realities as diametrically opposed, the 'whatness' suggests an underlying stratum of unqualified meaning, upon which our encounters play out in concert with the billions of encounters effected by previous generations. Simultaneously, the development by humans of complementary forms of artificial intelligence makes it impossible to conceive of reality as merely another invention, since the two conduct a large part of their relationship independently of our interference. Indeed, the strange encounter between the digital gaze and the 'whatness' may force us to confront a very different kind of reality than the one we have thus far experienced.

If we speak exclusively of the pre-digital human encounter, then Stephen Dedalus' two-pronged theory of the encounter works as a microcosm of an ongoing debate on aesthetics. On one side, the image is seen as inextricably bound up in our biological nature, our genetic material as a particular formula for decoding visual input into meaning. While Stephen imagines Darwinism as anathema to aesthetics (leading instead to eugenics), the root argument lives on in the biophilia theory of E.O. Wilson. He qualifies our encounter with the landscape as a deep-rooted form of 'savannah gestalt', in which we subconsciously desire, seek, and remake those biomes that recall the environment in which our ancestors first evolved bipedalism and other definitive traits for the modern human. At the same time, he explains our instinctive as well as cultural responses to threatening climates and organisms, such as hellfire or the serpent, as a deeply embedded biological response. The biophilia theory makes reality a savage battleground, using resonant images–visual and metaphorical, artistic and literary–to guide our animalistic nature against our 'better' judgment. The image becomes a weapon against the encroaching reality. Truth is not, in this case, the correlation between image and reality, but the survival of the fittest.

Stephen's second theory, that of the transcendent quality of the image (at least in terms of aesthetics, if not semantics) differs in its flow of causality. Art, as conceptual armature, precedes our animalistic adaption and represents a purer form of human consciousness. In fact, the cognitive appraisal of our surroundings as an imageable landscape is understood primarily as a creative act. This explanation recalls a section of Leonardo da Vinci's *A Treatise on Painting*, in which the artist describes 'a way to bring out the genius by various inventions' by looking at stained walls, piles of ashes, clouds, and rocky escarpments in order to find the complex forms and landscapes necessary to paint scenes (whether battlegrounds, faces, or 'monstrous things') of sufficient intricacy and diversity. (3) The counterpart to this active artistic technique is the more involuntary phenomenon of pareidolia or apophenia, (4) in which meaning and pattern are construed from ostensibly random fields of data. In this sense, reality is an amorphous soup that can only be organised and imbued with intention by the human power of creation. Leonardo celebrates this default state of chaos, saying that 'in confused things genius is aroused by new inventions' – as long as there is a precise understanding of the individual elements that inhabit it.

While the debate on the human aesthetic encounter, on a spectrum between hardwired response and aleatory creation, is still in play, the introduction of digital intelligence alters that polarity. Computer code grants us the privilege of directly witnessing the interaction of digital logic with mass quantities of numeric, lexical, or visual data. To that end, as the active 'evolvers' of digital intelligence, we condition its encounter based on the things we design it to look for. Initiatives like Google's DeepDream, which seeks and interprets dog faces (among other visual references) in any image fed to it, hint at the creative possibilities buried within that process, or at least the computer's potential to create 'art' for human eyes. Yet this understanding works mostly on our terms as creators and users of digital tools. To understand what the encounter means in terms of digital intelligence *for its own sake*, we require another framework – and we may find it, ironically, within art history itself.

In *Real Spaces*, the art historian David Summers constructs a lineage of art on two pivotal moments. The first moment is the invention of the image as a way of '[making] present in social spaces what for some reason is not present' physically: the hand-stencils and animal figures painted on cave walls in Sulawesi, El Castillo, and Chauvet in the Palaeolithic era are the earliest evidence of this cultural advance. Crucially, the invention of the image allowed humans to translate dynamic reality into static surfaces, making it possible to reorder the world through spatial hierarchies, frames, orders, ratios, symbols, and representational systems. Over the next thirty thousand years, the surface would develop an internal logic, absorbing technological innovations like the perspectival grid and propagating them through the circulation of artworks in the emerging global network.

Roughly one hundred years ago, however, as Joyce was developing *Portrait*, the ability of art to represent reality amid the overall context of technological and social progress met its reckoning. On one hand, the mechanical and chemical process of photography had become an accepted artistic form of systematically reproducing the visual evidence of reality; on the other, the nascent field of psychology questioned whether that evidence documented reality as such. At this point, the second moment arose, epitomised by René Magritte's *La trahison des images.* Below a painting of a pipe, Magritte writes the words 'Ceci n'est pas une pipe' –this is not a pipe. This work reveals a turning point: the image is no longer the conquest of reality. It is both a fantasy and a lie, a surface and a physical object.

In the intervening century, as the field of art underwent exponential diversification and expansion, it was far less concerned with the image as a tool for ordering and making sense of the world. At least, we *humans* were not. Computers, meanwhile, have an enormous affinity with the image. Their ability to swap meaningful interpretation with quantitative cataloguing allows for a massive increase in the amount of surfaces they can regard. At the same time, they can continuously apply their growing awareness and recognition of individual elements (as Leonardo suggested) to a sea of images without first developing a top-down explanation, something we humans can barely resist doing. While we continue to create and nourish ourselves with the human-generated images we deem valid as art, we are simultaneously devouring, submitting to, and re-enacting the image encounters of computers. What would it mean, on the other hand, if we made art for the digital gaze? If the algorithm has an aesthetic encounter, can it also undergo an epiphany?

In May of 2015, Richard Wentworth created the artwork *Agora* on the roof of a car park in Peckham, South London. A thick stroke of aluminium paint curves and squiggles across the entire concrete surface, the curiously useless border of an idiosyncratic zone, a children's maze without directionality. While a multitude of factors–human perspective, the fickle British weather, and the precarity of underused London property–may condition the ability of visitors to see *Agora* in person, (5) the work's natural viewing state may be through the form of the digital encounter, mapped in planimetric perfection through the aerial vision of Google

Earth. From this perspective, the digital gaze not only takes in the pleasingly precise turning radius of *Agora*, but also compares it to the round clusters of trees to the north and contrasts it with the orthogonal ordering of row house and warehouse roofs to the east and south. *Agora* will be a work continually reproduced as every cycle of satellite imagery documents its reflective lines, as long as the substratum of undisturbed car park remains.

In other views, this digital visual system also reveals dimensions of reality that our own eyes may obscure. Switch to bird's eye view and the virtual representation system of Google Earth stitches together the flat, distorted perspective of central Peckham with the three-dimensionally mapped agglomeration of the upper half of Southwark, continuing into the city. Along Commercial Way, Peckham Hill Street, and Goldsmith Road, the boundary between Peckham and the wards of Faraday, East Walsworth, and Livesey may not be immediately readable to the pedestrian, but the digital gaze both reveals that difference (of information? of technology? of power?) and gives it an aesthetic language. At the same time, it's worth seeing how *we*, the humans, fare from this perspective. At the aerial scale, we are too small to notice, but the panoramas taken at roof level show the bodies of humans in beguilingly surreal configurations. People vanish from the waist down, overlap each other, and morph through different scales from the left hand to the right hand of the body (the panoramic software does a decent Francis Bacon). In these images, we see the hint of a reality translated through a radically different aesthetic encounter; this time, however, *we* are fixed inside the amorphous reality, and the epiphany is purely in the digital.

(1) '...that, though the same object may not seem beautiful to all people, all people who admire a beautiful object find in it certain relations which satisfy and coincide with the stages themselves of all aesthetic apprehension. These relations of the sensible, visible to you through one form and to me through another, must be therefore the necessary qualities of beauty.'

(2) The change from the word 'symmetry' in Stephen Hero to 'harmony' in Portrait already suggests a loosening of the definition of beauty within Joyce's decade of work.

(3) Somewhat snidely, Leonardo even claims that 'as our Botticelli said, the study [of landscape painting] was in vain, because only by throwing a sponge dipped in diverse colours against a wall, it makes a stain in which one sees a beautiful landscape...but even if these blotches encourage inventions, they do not represent anything in particular. And that painter made very sad landscapes.'

(4) Apophenia refers to the interpretation of meaningful patterns in any kind of data, while pareidolia is strictly visual, often used to describe the detection of faces in landscapes or inanimate objects.

(5) Amusingly, some websites list the work as on view only until the end of September.

Horizontal and Vertical Exchange
Miraj Ahmed

As an artist and architect, I've always found it intriguing that the making and experience of art and architecture can be most potent in sites of decay and indeterminacy. This condition seems to offer a way to short circuit the problem of the preconceived image, whereby the indeterminate space offers chance, risk and presence. Art has always adorned buildings and public spaces as a way of mediating and shaping our cultural identities. We are familiar with architecture that is specifically designed for art and vice versa–from religious buildings and palaces to museums and galleries. But the most ordinary buildings in an incomplete or obsolete state seem to acquire a strange spatial poetry and mythic quality that stirs the imagination. Ruin causes a visceral experience of space that seduces artists to make temporal art in a way that 'bespoke' spaces do not. It is this state of estrangement that has inspired Hannah Barry and Bold Tendencies to commission temporary art interventions, performances and Frank's Cafe in the disused Peckham car park since 2007. An 'other' place to perform culture–free from notions of 'gallery' or 'museum'–it has become a kind of cultural laboratory. Recently, a drawn intervention Agora by Richard Wentworth has become the first commission to remain permanently.

'Agora' is a collection of roof-scape lines experienced as a culmination of a journey through thresholds from the streets of Peckham, through empty parking levels to the top of the building – Level 10. On arrival, a new journey of discovery begins. However, it is important to first describe the street and intermediate levels, as this sets the context for the work.

Rye Lane is a diverse streetscape, set within one of those lively, working-class, multicultural communities that London does, or used to do, so well. The area has a history of decline and deprivation that has left a patina on the urban fabric; railway viaducts, light industry and a stock of Georgian or Victorian terraces intermingled with postwar council housing. The multi-storey car park, council-owned and built in the 1980s, is part of this townscape. Its power lies not only in its dereliction and emptiness, but also our mental image-bank of such spaces. From Piranesi to the many cinematic garage scenes (such as 'Get Carter', 1971), the ruin and the incomplete have been a romantic pursuit within art and architecture articulated through a variety of imaginative narratives.

Ignasi de Solà-Morales described such spaces in his 1995 essay 'Terrain Vague', identifying the role of postwar photography – particularly that of the 1970s – in revealing the potentiality of abandoned, derelict urban buildings.

> 'The relationship between the absence of use, of activity, and the sense of freedom, of expectancy, is fundamental to understanding all the evocative potential that the city's terrains vagues have accrued as part of the perception of the city in recent years. Void, then, as

absence, and yet also as promise, as encounter, as the space of the possible, expectation.' (1)

The postwar 'wasteland' of unproductive, redundant space was the condition that led to so much art and culture in Britain. Solà-Morales saw that art could engage easily with such 'terrains vagues.' But he also asked how architecture, with its natural relation to order, function and desire for productive space, might act within such spaces without overpowering them. This is the problem with which the Bold Tendencies project has been grappling – freedom to create an open public space with civic value, in the face of the pressures of land value and development potential.

The original Peckham carpark designers made some attempts to fit into the site and 'beautify' it's exterior with cosmetic geometric forms and brick detailing, but once inside, it is unrepentantly raw. The carpark connects into the circuitry of the city; as a building it is immediately infrastructural. Unlike railway stations that are quite public, the carpark deals with compartmentalised private cars, setting up a strangely alienating relation with its users. It is utilitarian, tough and ruthlessly brutal – we don't expect it to be pretty. The carpark is the 20th century 'type', a bare Corbusian 'Domino House'. Land and roadway stacked up.

Its geometry is determined by horizontality, incline and turning circles, all derived from the movement of the car. I was always struck by the artistic potential of the Architects Data by Ernst

Neufert, with its metric diagrams of ergonomics and efficiency or parking. Car parks seem to be the purest representations of these kinds of drawings. As spaces for movement and temporary stasis, the car park lends itself to the display of art–Wright's Guggenheim comes to mind. Bold Tendencies' use of the spaces pre-dates Herzog and De Meuron's 111 Lincoln Road project in Miami, which also explores the hidden potentials of multi-storey carparks. The geometry sets certain challenges, its horizontality, the low ceilings, deep plan, the ramps, low light levels. The expansive flow of space and its robustness lends itself to the possibilities of art and also music, performance and other forms of gathering.

> 'A return to reality does not imply any new acceptances, but means that one is seduced in a base manner, without transpositions and to the point of screaming, opening his eyes wide: opening them wide, then, before a big toe.' (2)

Moving through through the layers of expansive intermediate floor plates, we experience a heightened sense of perspectival compression and feel vulnerable–not just because of the car park's material atmosphere, but also because of the images stored in our heads. With its utilitarian concrete, the car park is, after George Bataille, 'the big toe' of architecture (alluding to a kind of baseness where there is no ideal and all is fluid). Indeed, the building was once poured into shape. The spaces have a cave like beauty both visual and aural, and they offer themselves to an honest and guttural response from the artist.

And finally to the top level to be moved another way by Richard Wentworth's large painted lines on the floor. It is called 'Agora', alluding to a notion of ground. In a sense, it is what the carpark has become – a civic occupation of ground, a gathering place for cultural exchange. The lines of circulation move 'round as though following an elegant, magical vehicular dance. The immediate tendency is to follow them to see where they lead – is it one line or several, how do they connect, where do they lead? Almost meeting but never crossing, the lines in their entirety seem to physically map a territory, negotiating the 'lay of the land', and also the relationship of the car park to our surroundings. There is a strong sense that the work relates to the body in the way they were made, the choreography of lines and occupation of available space – just over half of the roof.

Both playful and serious, Agora is a purposeful scribble made of stuff we normally find on roofs; namely, aluminium waterproofing paint. Its materiality has a liquid quality that plays with light, sometimes reflecting, sometimes invisible, losing and finding oneself in relation to the locale. At times, the lines lead our gaze to the spectacular panoramic cityscape. The intervention gathers in the environment from all directions. In meandering across the roof, it occurred to me that as a by-product of this very site-specific act at this scale in the city, the aluminium 'traces' of Agora would surely be seen from space and appear on a satellite image.

Here is a kind of urban 'geoglyph' in London that appears on Google Earth, which therefore becomes another way of understanding the work: a global perception aided by space technology and digital media. Indeed, one can see in the satellite image the extent of the lines and their relation to the surrounding roof surfaces. In this view, the markings have a certain graphic quality akin to architectural notations that refer to the organic–trees or water. But there is a deeper phenomenon at play, to do with the act of making lines the ground on a geographic scale. Humans have always cherished the ability to look down on earth, which can be attributed to our experience of landscape, both empirically and conceptually. Empirically because we have lived in trees, up mountains and looked down–more recently from aircraft and satellites, but conceptually through the ability to project our minds to the sight of birds or the gods. Wentworth's 'Agora' joins the family of geoglyphs - geographic marks of ancient chalk downs, the Nazca lines, desire lines. The seemingly random act of roaming and wandering as a process of 'getting to know' relates very much to that ancient instinct, to survey with the body as the instrument. The horizontal act of engaging with ground in this way connects us vertically to whoever is 'up there'. But ultimately it is us looking down–getting to understand where we are. Agora registers us in Peckham horizontally and vertically.

In a world saturated with images, whereby our experience is constantly mediated, Wentworth's work is about presence and lived experience. A gathering of observations about the relationships between things, our bodies and the peculiarities of the world around us that reveal certain behaviours. His work deals with physicality and relationship between materials, space and the hidden choreographies that are proportional, cultural and political. Agora engages the found roof surface of Peckham Carpark just as a doodle engages a page or an abstract painting a canvas – a contemplative corporeal exploration that negotiates its spaces and edges, its local conditions to be experienced live and in-situ, but which are connected globally.

(1) Ignasi de Solá Morales Rubió 'Terrain Vague' from Anyplace (Cynthia Davidson), Cambridge MA: MIT Press, 1995, p.118–123

(2) George Bataille Visions of Excess: Selected Writings 1929–1939

When Art Exitis the Gallery
Attilia Fattori Franchini (AFF) interviewed by Jack Self (JS)

JS
You have worked as the curator for two of the three projects in this exhibition. How did you first become involved with Bold Tendencies?

AFF
I have known Hannah (Barry) and the Bold Tendencies programme for a number of years, although I came to understand its relationship to Peckham in a new way when I started studying at nearby Goldsmiths University in 2009. At that time, and still now, the car park was a place where a certain community of artists were able to experiment, and many of my artistic friends had a connection to the site.

Bold Tendencies has always struck me as an exceptional event; it is a normal urban site that every summer is transformed into a visual arts centre. This condition of being outside the normal framework means that exhibitions are able happen in a more loose way than within institutions, and within a panorama of personal interests in London they really stand out.

Last winter Hannah contacted me. She was basically restructuring the way Bold Tendencies existed, both as a visual art initiative and in the form of the commissioned works. Around December she asked me to get involved – it was short timing for a project of that size, for a site of that kind.

JS
Had you been involved with Metahaven and åyr before? What drew you specifically to these artists?

AFF
There were three aspects that particularly attracted me to these artists, none of whom I had worked with previously (although I held their work in high esteem). The first aspect was that they do not represent individuals; Metahaven is a duo and åyr is a collective. Secondly, neither belongs precisely within the field of visual art; they come with a certain knowledge that is parallel to the visual arts. Thirdly, their work deals with many of the conditions of contemporary life that also influence the site itself.

JS
As you say, the site is highly particular and requires quite a unique curatorial approach. Amongst the other categories you've mentioned, these artists are also known for how they address certain qualities of space and spatial practice.

AFF
I was interested in commissioning someone who could contextualise the site and make use of it from a spatial point of view, which was certainly part of the interest in working with people who do not approach their work from a pure visual art context.

I was keen to avoid the commission simply resulting in the placement of sculptures in a car park. I wanted someone who could engage with the space and its unusual conditions, and to therefore create a space that could be transformative for the public. I was really interested in Metahaven and åyr because they have a broader political, cultural and spatial understanding of reality as it applies to art. Metahaven approach art from a graphic design and branding background, while åyr do so from an architectural perspective. They do think about conditions of space, but more importantly they consider how the political dimension of that space is involved and invoked in the work.

From a curatorial point of view, I tried to facilitate the work by giving the artists a carte blanche, at the same time asking them to think about the space and their involvement with it.

I think both artists dealt with the space fantastically. At a primary level their interventions reinforced the existing structure, rather than trying to create an artificial context. Metahaven used the floor plane to display scarf textiles in a grid, through a shipping palette structure that evolved through time. åyr used the car park ceiling to determine the placement of large light boxes. These partitions create intimate spaces through the passage of the car park, which completely transforms the viewer's experience.

JS

When we use the expression 'site-specific installation,' often the understanding of that 'site' is very similar to what you've just described, in terms of how the work reinforces or subverts certain aspects of the immediate context of where it is displayed. But I want to come back to the idea that the 'site' also includes the entire car park, the context of Peckham, the urban context of London (which may or may not be indicative of the global city) and finally even the context of the contemporary art world.

AFF

The artworks certainly responded very consciously to the broader context, perhaps more directly from åyr than Metahaven. Possessed is more concerned with a discussion of broader digital culture – the iPhone, quick communication, Snapchat – and the virtual condition in general.

In the case of åyr, they spent lots of time in the area itself, using 'readymade' elements from Peckham in their work. The images presented on the light boxes may not be representative of the current state of Peckham, but they speak to certain domestic aspirations that others hold for this place. They organised collaborations for the reverse of the boxes with a project space, a writer and a primary school. These groups responded to their work, which aimed to understand how the community perceives the car park, and how the community around the car park has also been changing as a result of precisely these kinds of artistic initiatives. What I also wanted to highlight was that Bold Tendencies is itself a cause of gentrification in Peckham – for both good and bad. It has brought a transformation that is now pushing out the local communities from the area. Cultural spaces of almost any kind have effects on rental rates and the property market, in an escalating cycle that is well known. This fundamentally changes the way communities have been living for a long time. åyr definitely tapped into these conditions quite critically, as they tried to understand this change to the local community.

JS
Given this situation, as a curator, did you have a specific audience in mind with whom you wanted to communicate?

AFF
I definitely wanted to communicate first with the local audience, the general public, and then the art world. For the general public, I was really thinking of the possibility of a transformative experience with the work when passing through it, and having the possibility of both a superficial or deeper relation depending on their engagement. For an art audience, I imagined how to prompt a reflection on their vision of contemporary London, in a way exposing the problems we're all facing as inhabitants.

I think I'm really suggesting, in different ways, that the city has changed and is no longer concentrating on its inhabitants. London has sold its soul. London has sold its soul to urban developers and estate agents. Exposing these elements by placing art works into such a hybrid site was quite important, and part of the goal of the commission and my work as a facilitator. That's why I chose artists that are quite political in the work they do.

JS
The Bold Tendencies show came before certain events, like the architectural collective Assemble winning the Turner Prize. Do you think the art world, and curatorial practice particularly, is beginning to rethink the role of political art in the city, in new and more pronounced ways?

AFF
I have two theories about this. One is: definitely yes. It's a slow transformation, however specific moments–as with Assemble winning the Turner Prize–are reinforcing a more general phenomenon of architecture and the process of 'design' being placed into an art context. These frequently concern the role of social and political conditions in shaping urban space. They are also responsible for highlighting the profound contradictions that frame our experience of this so-called 'global city.'

On the other hand, art is definitely a factor in driving the expansion of our cities, and a certain kind of city that is no longer in communication with any local communities. In a way, self-reflection and self-guilt is always somewhat political, or explores political subjects, while remaining self-referential to an artistic context.

JS
Is that how it should be?

AFF
From my perspective, we should be more responsible about what we place in artistic

contexts. Artworks can support the way we understand reality. Art can be transformative, which is a word I use quite a lot. But I really believe that; if you are an artist and you have the power to expose an idea to different kinds of audiences, be careful what you say.

JS
This proposal might seem in some ways very easy to accept, but it is also quite a radical proposition to hear from someone in your position, in comparison even with five years ago.

AFF
Completely. It's also perhaps a product of my thinking about recent changes in the art market. In the last three years the art market has turned itself into an investment field. Previously, there were distinct financial sectors outside the art world and gallery system: stock markets, real estate markets, foreign exchange and other financial markets. Slowly, they transformed contemporary art into a place for specialised traders. A lot of work owes its existence to its role in the circulation of art and its price as a commodity. A lot of the work is informed by the exchange of visual images, and the bubble created to promote this process has in fact created a lot of empty works (whose 'value' has been completely inflated by the market).

In this context, the political, social and particularly economic state of art today has become extremely relevant. I believe in art. It is a social necessity, not a financial commodity. I want to facilitate cultural thinking and reflection on these issues, more than just accelerating the circulation of an image base whose only purpose is to artificially inflate value.

JS
That's very powerful as a position.

AFF
Well! Of course it is not easy, or possible, to always pursue this extreme view. But seriously: fuck the market.

JS
For me, as an outsider and as an architect, the art world seems at times exhausted.

AFF
Exactly. In order to fuel this constant growth, we are reaching a state of exhaustion. The art world is homogenising on a global scale while at the same time there are a million art fairs, a million biennials. You're always on a plane, as a human condition it's not right. That's why space is again becoming a key factor, because you feel displaced.

JS
I'm very interested by creative fields that have been heavily financialised, which always results in extremely rigid production cycles. The world of fashion is a case in point. There's an increasingly severe system of annual deadlines for creative production, although this was not the case until very recently. Does this have some relation to what is happening in art?

AFF

Completely. The more mainstream a field becomes, the more increased production and economies of scale become crucial. We don't like to say it, but art is the creative product at the core of this system. The best strategy to resist this exploitation of art-as-a-product is in fact through the subject of the art itself. We should perhaps add, this entire logic used to be a particularly Western tradition. At its worst, the commodification of art was in effect bouncing back and forth across the Atlantic. The pressure for every gallery today is to be a global gallery, connected to this international network. The content of art has become largely an economic question, from a market perspective.

The point is that within this system the circulation of the image of the work comes before the work itself, which drives a concentration of the characteristics of the image. There's a whole category of image-making which looks a lot like art, and is exchanged like art, but is not art.

JS

Absolutely. This explains perhaps why the art market has become so highly risk-averse. There is still political art being produced, maybe even more than ever, but it is always in precise equilibrium. The work in many contemporary galleries seems to be a form of spread betting: every category of contemporary art is present simultaneously, and carefully represented in proportion to its current popularity.

AFF
It has been striking to see the decline of video works exhibited in the context of Art Fairs. The mainstream approach leans towards 2D works, which are collectables also easier to trade. This is really different from why I got involved in art. This is not to demonise 2D practitioners whatsoever; there are different forms of art that are not always sellable, and these can be powerful and interesting. In London, aside from the Serpentine Gallery, which has a strong public programme, there are not very many venues that are pursuing performance art. There are so few sound events. We have to support at every level, experimentation with forms that are less physical or which are ephemeral.

Outside institutions it is almost impossible to sell video works, for example, because they don't enter into the five-year investment cycle.

I have tried with the Bold Tendencies commissions to turn this quite dramatic situation into a positive. How can I promote and explore hybrid models of art? This is also an economic question: how can artists engaged in experimental practice be supported financially when they're not exhibiting content for acquisition? How can my role as a curator be to expand this discourse?

JS
I don't see this as contradictory. Resistance or rejection of conditions we find unacceptable must begin as a critical act, although it can never end there. However, the positive proposition is often formulated as a response.

To conclude: the Bold Tendencies exhibition for 2015 has now closed. I want to ask you what your own reflections on this process have been, and on the exhibition itself.

AFF

Good question. I will answer it quite informally and personally, if I may. It has been a very peculiar project for me. I've never worked in public site of this genre. I have no frame of reference for a context that is so open. As a curator, you're really aware that the context significantly informs the perception of the artwork, and you need to create that context for the artwork to flourish and take on new meanings. For me, curating the Bold Tendencies project has been a massive challenge–from an organisational point of view, but also as I had to protect the artists and their work. I had to be sure that the context I created was correct, and I felt I didn't have full control. It wasn't a gallery; it wasn't a museum. It was a hybrid site.

There are a lot of things I've learnt from this project, principally how to support artists in contexts that are really difficult to define or understand, and how to ensure the right place for their works. After that, I have a million things I would do differently next time. Everything in the car park is highly at risk. The context is one where there is a bar on the roof. Not everyone that passes through the space is there because of an interest in the artworks. They're passing by, and sometimes they can be very disrespectful towards the artworks; they touch them, they step on them. Metahaven's work had been damaged on almost a weekly basis, as people walked on the glass. Metahaven were really tense about it, with very good reason. They wanted to know why the hell people are walking on the artworks? And we all asked ourselves the same question.

But it is not an art context; the bar upstairs is a Campari bar, and people are drunk on Campari. Defining the limits of control, and understanding how different audiences assimilated this context was a challenge. The gallery forms the way we engage with art. So one must be super aware of the critical framework and contextualisation of the work. This question was never fully resolved, partly because this negotiation of exposure and risk is integral to the site itself and the nature of the exhibition.

After all, this is what happens when art exists the gallery.

Biographies

Miraj Ahmed is a practising painter and architect. He has taught at the Architectural Association in London since 2000, is Associate Lecturer at Camberwell College of Art and was previously a Design Fellow at the University of Cambridge. His work focuses on several recurring themes rooted in his interest in spatiality and perception, particularly subtle subversions of ordinary objects and space. His ongoing *Heterotopia* series brings together notions of 'otherness' within familiar objects that allude to the body.

åyr is an art collective based in London whose work focuses on interiors, domesticity, internet and the city. It was founded by Fabrizio Ballabio, Alessandro Bava, Luis Ortega Govela, and Octave Perrault in 2014 to take part in the Venice Architecture Biennale as the Airbnb Pavilion. åyr are not endorsed by or affiliated with Airbnb Inc or any other Airbnb group company. Their work has appeared at Frieze Art Fair in London, and their texts have been published in Rhizome, Volume and the Harvard Design Magazine.

Bold Tendencies is a not-for-profit commissioning organisation that since 2007 has transformed a disused multi-storey car park in Peckham each year through its summer programme of visual art, architecture, music, theatre, film, literature, food and drink. The organisation aims to be nimble and responsive to varied audiences, creating immersive experiences and inspiring change. Bold Tendencies are proud of the key role they have played in the cultural and economic uplift of the area and as a launch pad for many successful careers in the creative industries.

Shumi Bose is an editor, teacher and curator based in London. Shumi was a curatorial collaborator for the 2012 Venice Biennale of Architecture, where she edited *Common Ground: A Critical Reader* with Sir David Chipperfield. She co-curated the 2016 British Pavilion at the Venice Biennale with Jack Self and Finn Williams. Shumi was previously Senior Editor for Blueprint Magazine, and is currently Senior Lecturer in Architectural History and Theory at Central Saint Martins College in London.

Federico Campagna is an Italian anarchist and author who writes on a range of subjects including anti-work, individualist anarchism and radical atheism. In 2009, Campagna began collaboration with Franco Berardi, whose reader he is editing. Campagna's first book, *The Last Night: Anti-Work, Atheism, Adventure* was published in 2013 by Zero Books. Campagna also regularly publishes online on Through Europe, a multilingual website including works from a range of contemporary writers.

Attilia Fattori Franchini is an independent curator based in London, responsible for commissioning åyr and Metahaven at the 2015 Bold Tendencies exhibition. Between 2013 and 2014 she curated *The Basement* at Paradise Row, London, a parallel programme dedicated to young unrepresented artists. Fattori Franchini's work explores networked cultures and the creation of hybrid platforms for the production and display of art. She is also co-founder of the online platforms bubblebyte.org and OpeningTimes and is currently part of Seventeen Gallery in London.

Suzanne Hall is an urban ethnographer, and has practised as an architect in South Africa. Her research and teaching interests include social and economic forms of inclusion and exclusion in the context of global urbanisation, and she currently focuses on the micro-economies and spaces of urban migration. Suzi is a recipient of the LSE's Robert McKenzie Prize for outstanding PhD research and the Rome Scholarship in Architecture. Her research monograph, *City, Street and Citizen: The measure of the ordinary*, was published in 2012.

Metahaven is a studio for design and research, founded by Vinca Kruk and Daniel van der Velden. Metahaven's work – both commissioned and self-directed – reflects political and social issues in collaboratively produced graphic design objects. Solo exhibitions include Stadtstaat (Künstlerhaus Stuttgart/Casco, 2009) and Islands in the Cloud (MoMA PS1, New York, 2013). Their latest book is *Black Transparency* (Sternberg Press, 2015), which joins *Uncorporate Identity*, on politics and visual identity (Lars Müller, 2010) and *Can Jokes Bring Down Governments* (Strelka Press, 2012), amongst others.

Jack Self is an architect and writer based in London. He is Director of the REAL foundation and Editor-in-Chief of its flagship magazine, the Real Review. He co-curated *Home Economics*, the 2016 British Pavilion at the Venice Biennale and his writing has appeared in *The Guardian*, *New Philosopher*, *032c*, and on CNN and the BBC. His first book was *Real Estates: Life Without Debt* (Bedford Press 2014), now in its second printing. Jack is Contributing Editor for the Architectural Review magazine.

The Real Estate Architecture Laboratory (REAL) is a cultural foundation and architectural institute. REAL recognises architecture as a common concern. REAL makes transparent the forces shaping our cities. REAL promotes alternative models of ownership. REAL believes in spatial equality and civic freedom. REAL insists on building as the means to an end. REAL engages positively with those in power. REAL aims to influence how and where we live, and the conditions of that life.

Tamar Shafrir is a writer and designer based in Genoa, Italy. She is cofounder of Space Caviar and previously received her master's degree in contextual design from the Design Academy Eindhoven. Her articles have been published in *Domus* magazine, and she was the editor of the catalogue for the first Istanbul Design Biennial. She has co-curated exhibitions as part of experimentadesign in Lisbon and the Shenzhen & Hong Kong Bi-City Biennale of Urbanism Architecture.

Richard Wentworth is a British artist, curator and teacher. He has played a leading role in New British Sculpture since the end of the 1970s. His work, encircling the notion of objects and their use as part of our day-to-day experiences, has altered the traditional definition of sculpture as well as photography. Richard's ongoing photographic series *Making Do and Getting By* (Koenig Books, 2015) documents the everyday, paying attention to objects, occasional and involuntary geometries as well as uncanny situations that often go unnoticed.

Possessed, Metahaven (detail of Grey Non-Market)

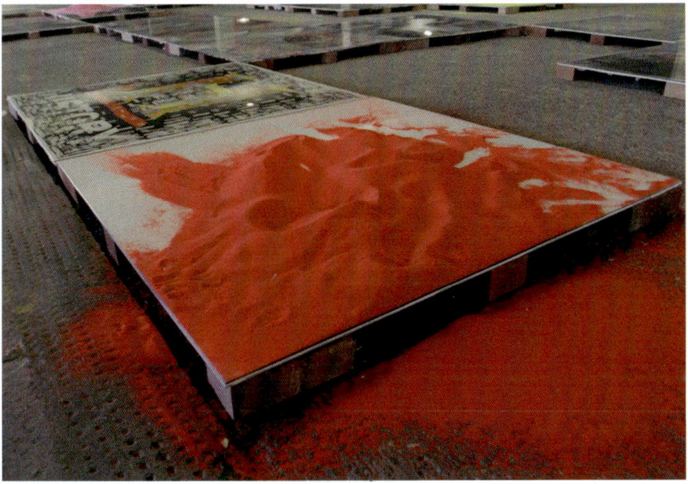

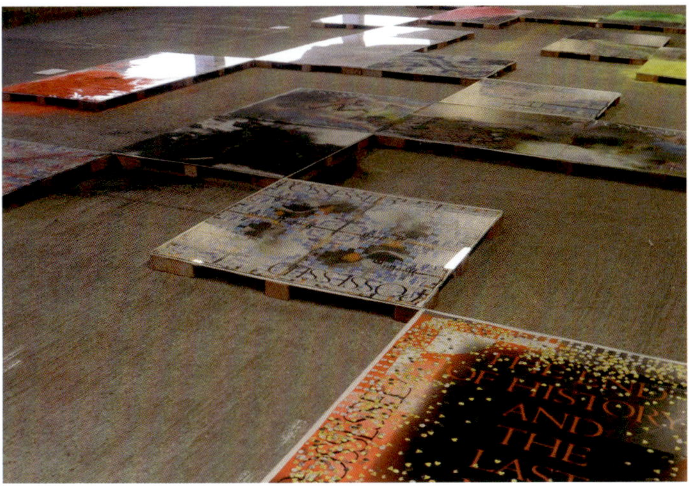

Possessed, Metahaven (detail of Grey Non-Market)

Possessed, Metahaven (Grey Non-Market)

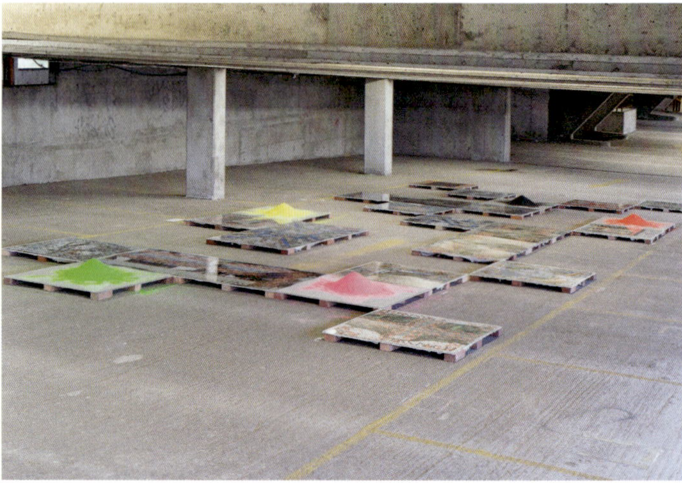

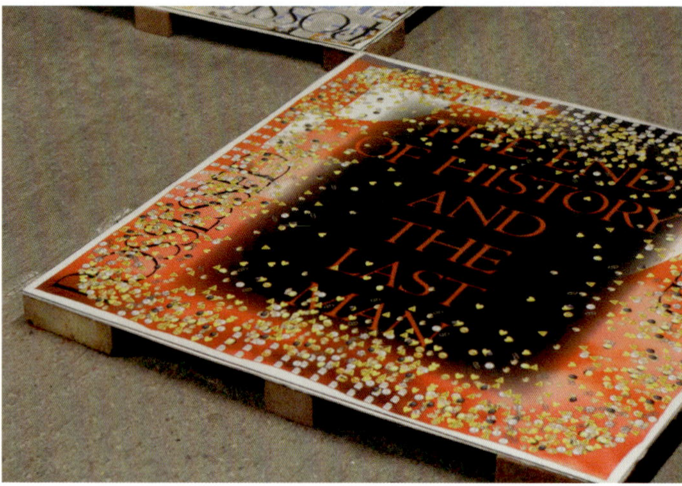

Possessed, Metahaven (detail of Grey Non-Market)

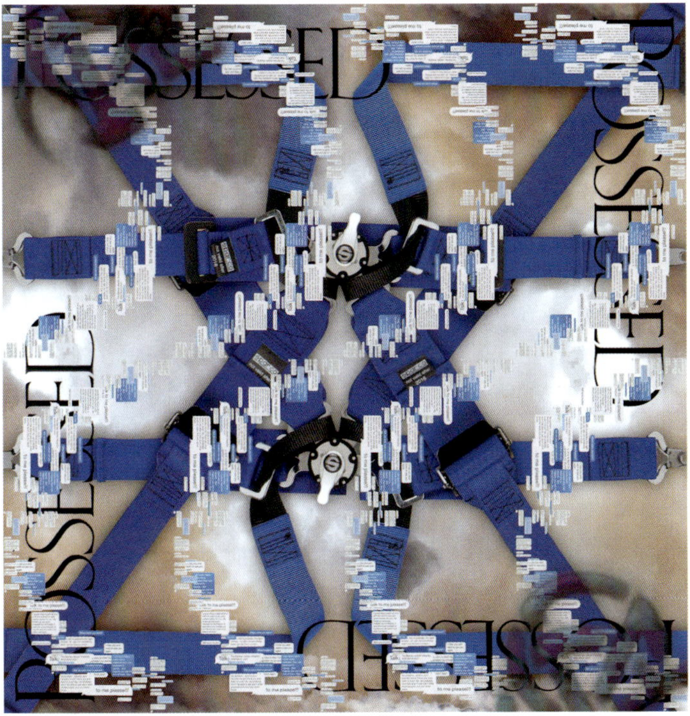

Possessed, Metahaven (Bluebelts scarf)

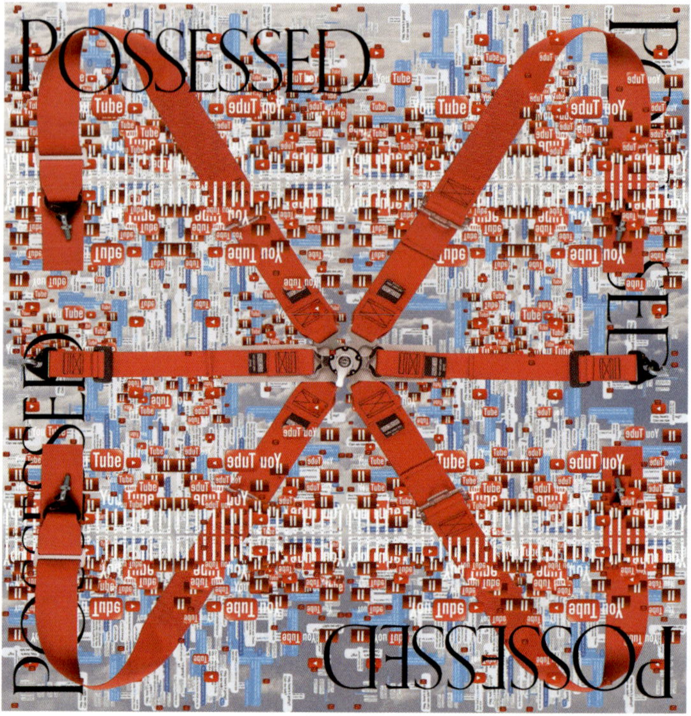

Possessed, Metahaven (Redbelts scarf)

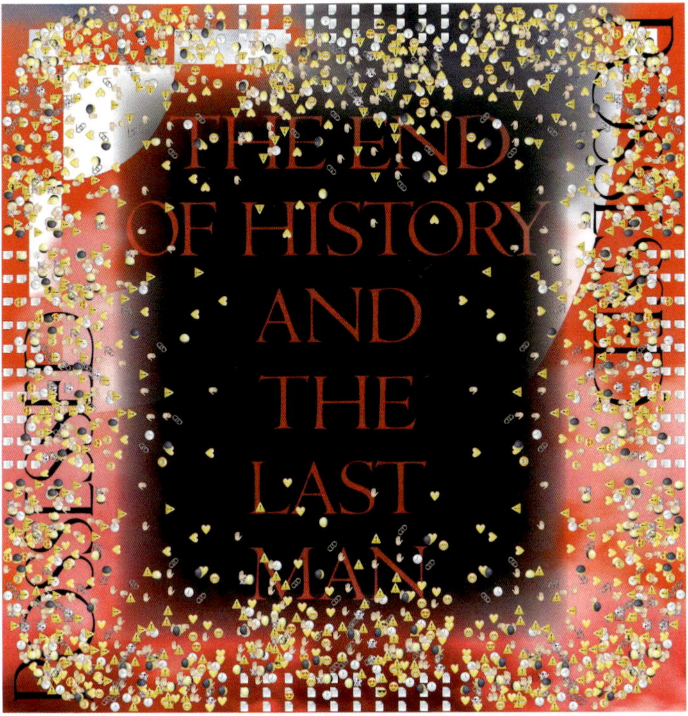

Possessed, Metahaven (History scarf)

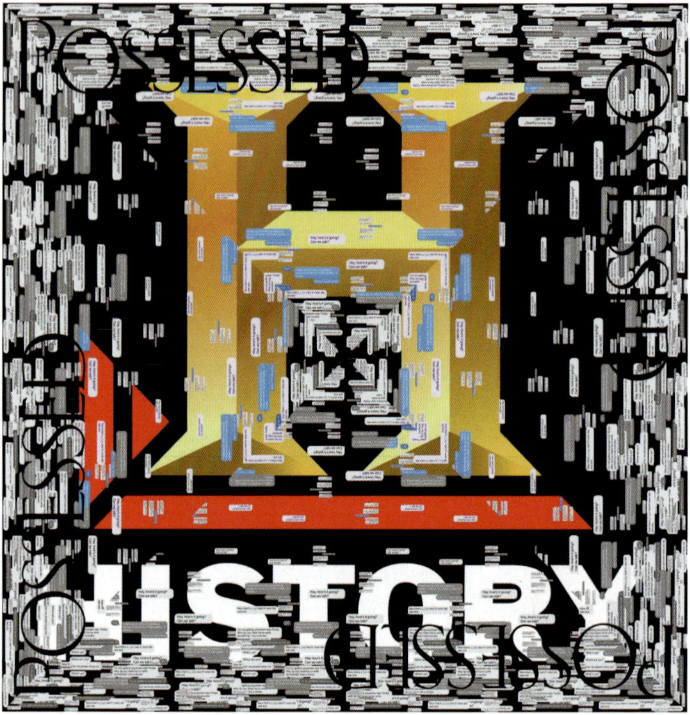

Possessed, Metahaven (History scarf)

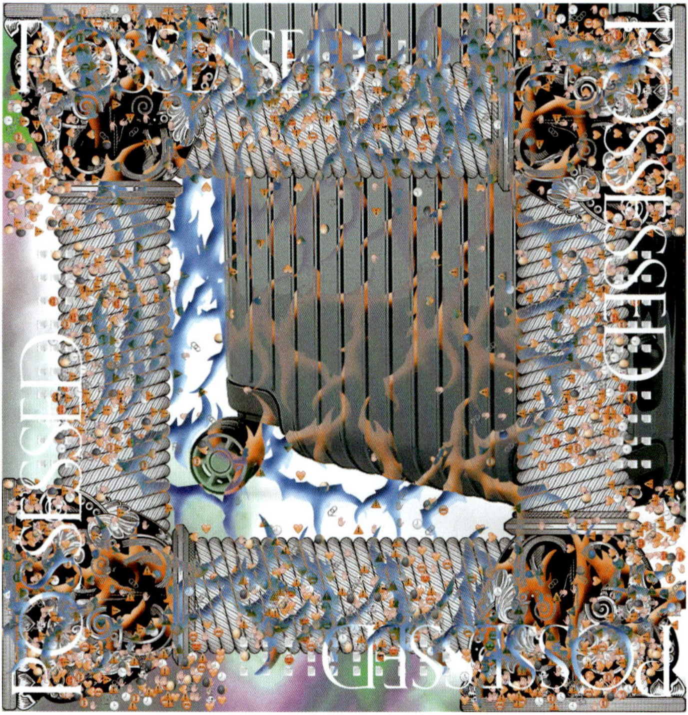

Possessed, Metahaven (Nomadic scarf)

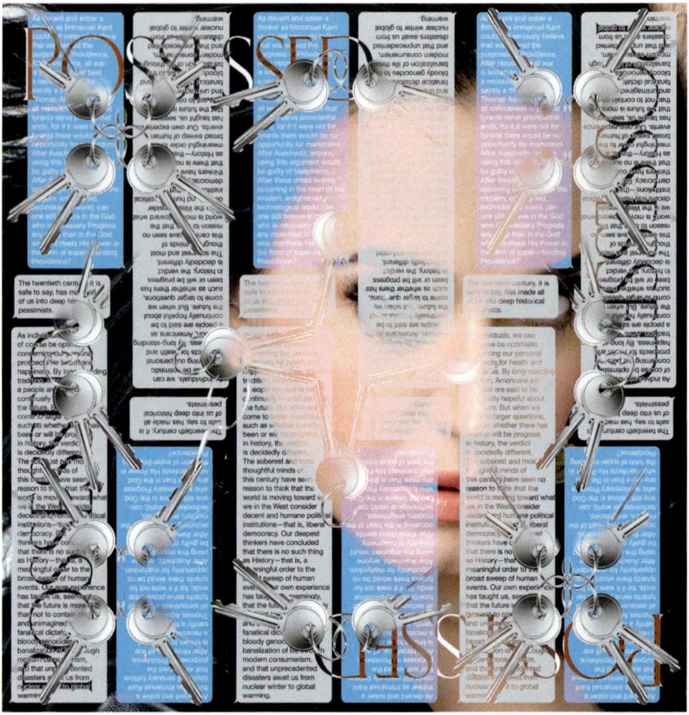

Possessed, Metahaven (Pessimists scarf)

Aspects of Change, åyr (looking South)

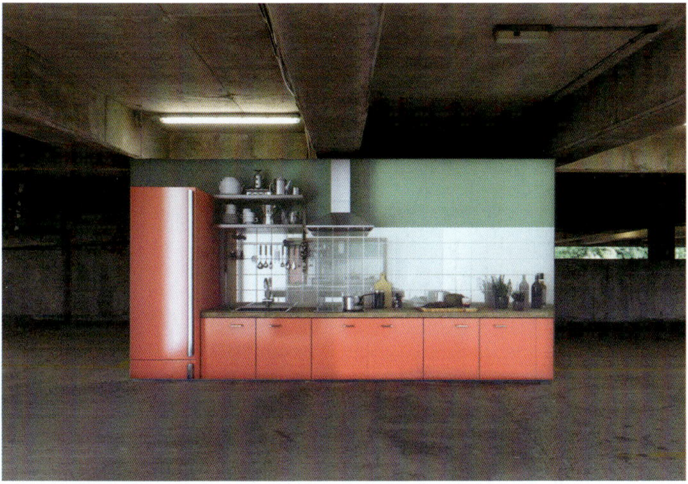

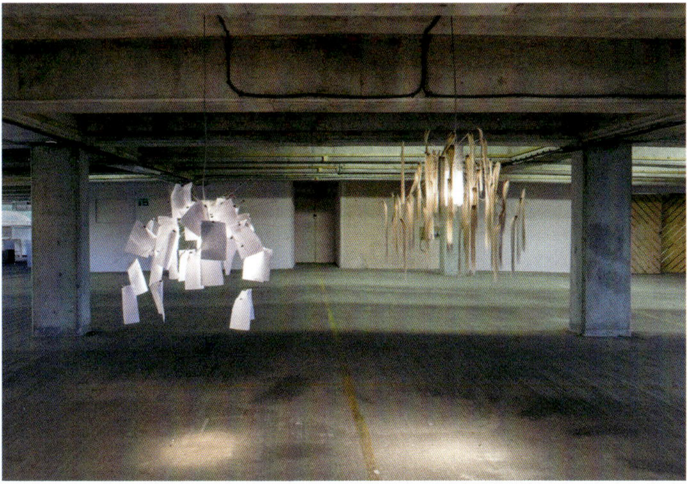

Aspects of Change, åyr (detail of chandeliers)

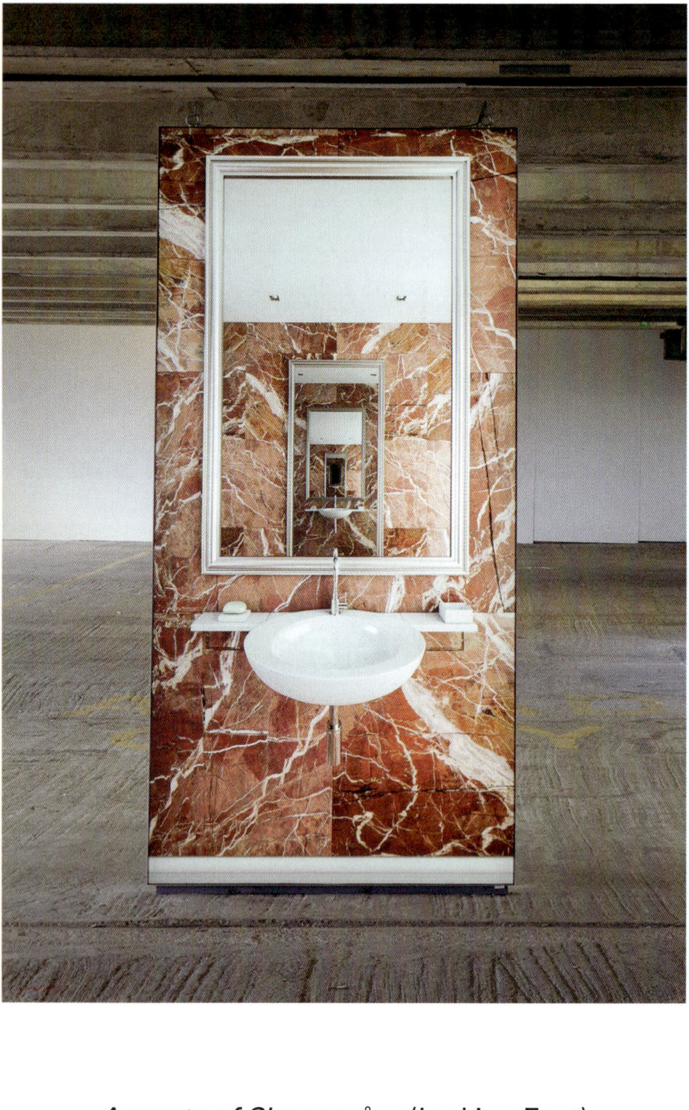

Aspects of Change, åyr (looking East)

Aspects of Change, åyr (looking North)

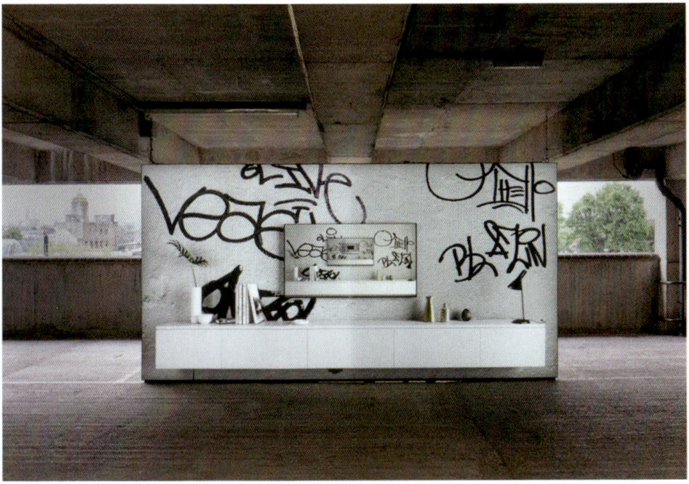

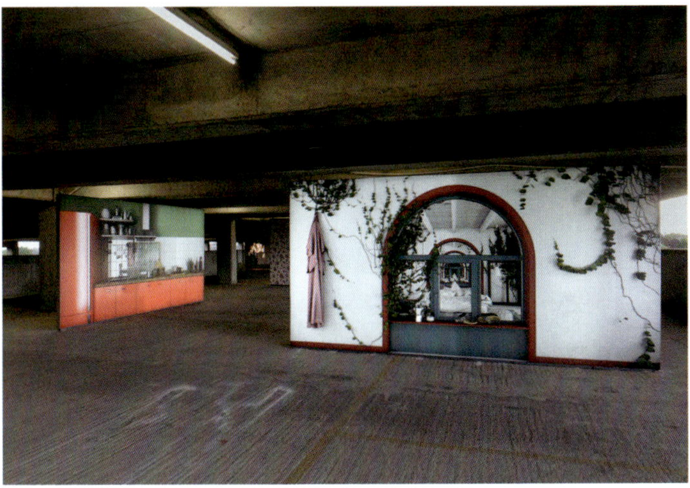

Aspects of Change, åyr (Southwest corner)

Aspects of Change, åyr (looking West)

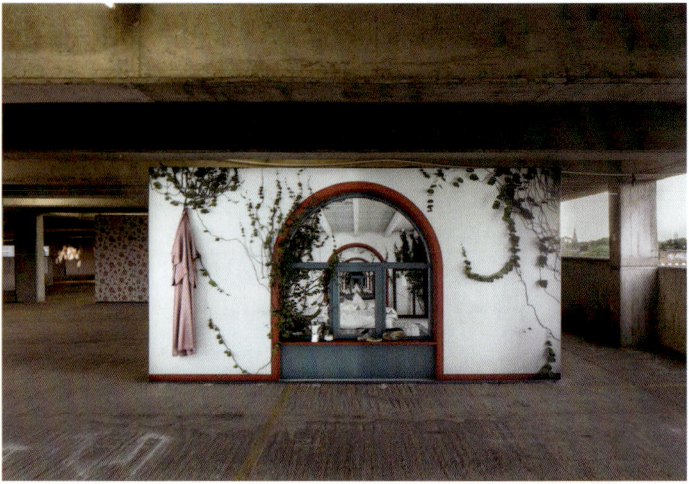

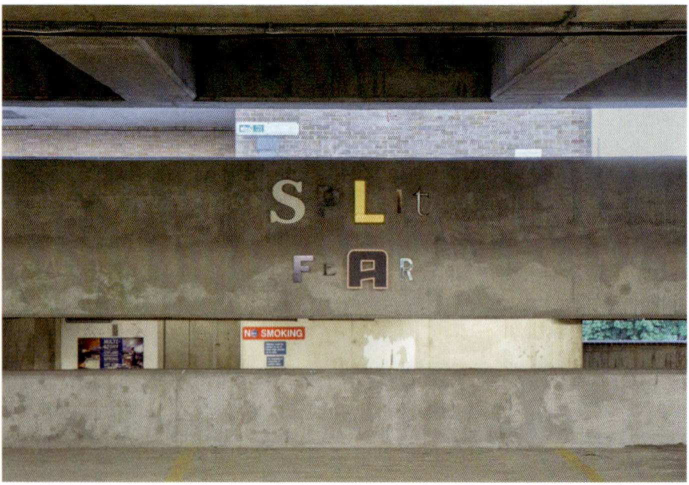

Aspects of Change, åyr (detail of Split Fear)

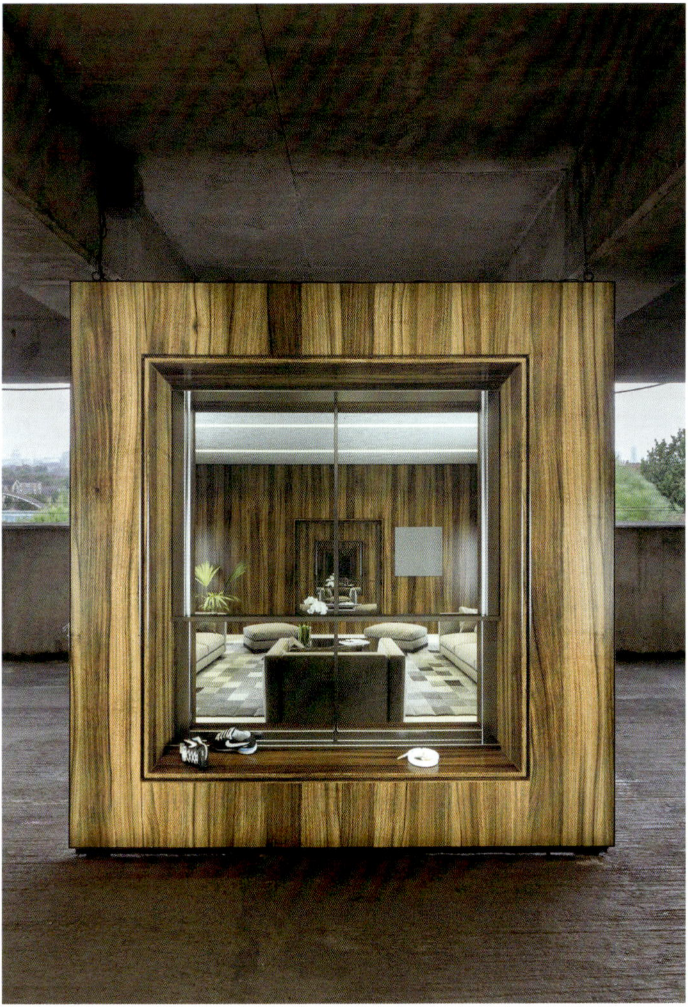

Aspects of Change, åyr (looking South)

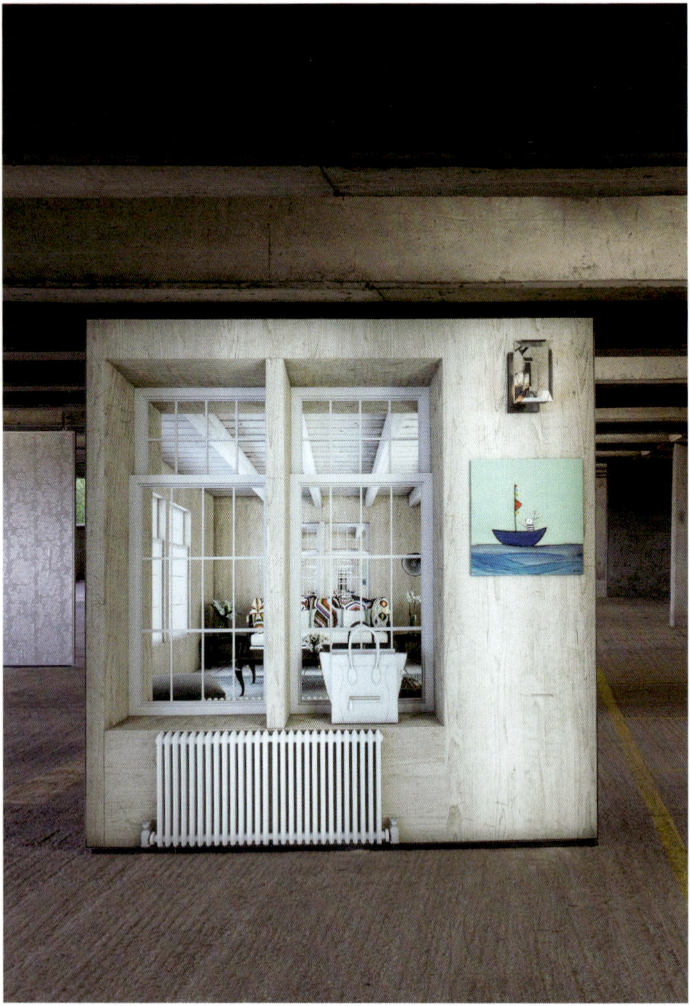

Aspects of Change, åyr (looking East)

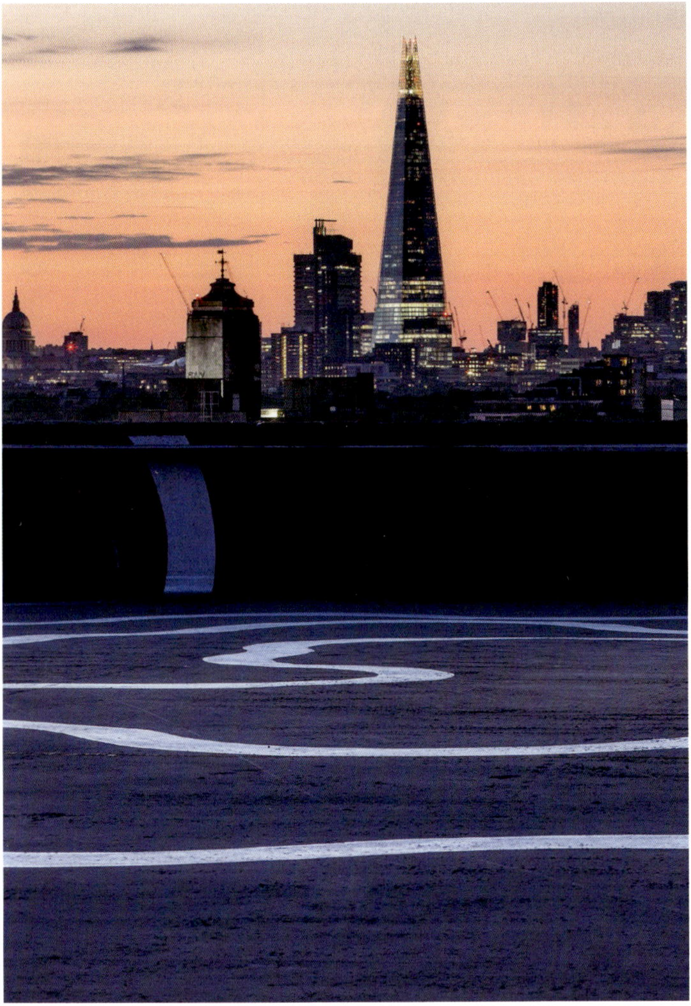

Agora, Richard Wentworth (toward the City)

Agora, Richard Wentworth (looking North)

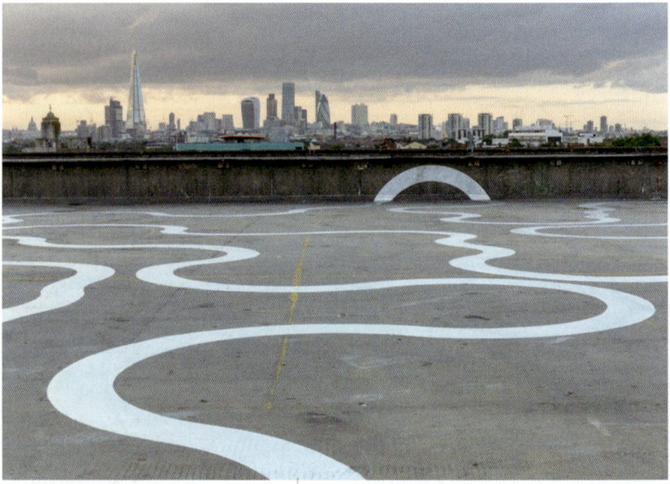

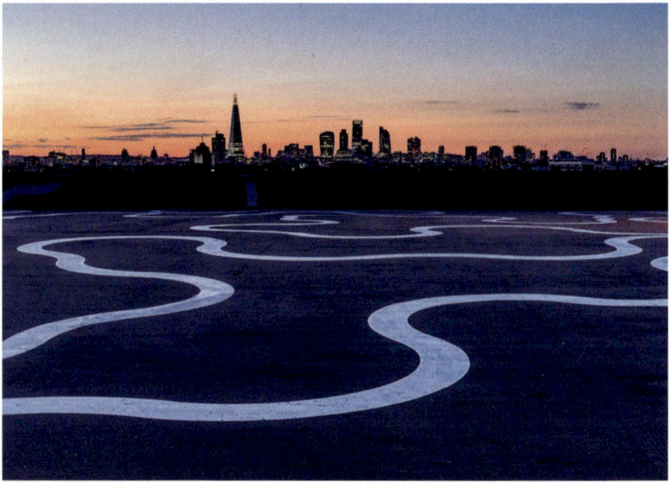

Agora, Richard Wentworth (by night)